Business Management

ANTHONIA O. CLARK Ph.D
Vocational & Technical Education Department
Faculty of Education
University of Benin, Benin City,
Edo State, Nigeria.

Published 2012 by arima publishing
www.arimapublishing.com

ISBN 978 1 84549 543 5
© Dr A.O. Clark 2012

Printed and bound in the United Kingdom

Typeset in Garamond 11/14

Swirl is an imprint of arima publishing.

arima publishing
ASK House, Northgate Avenue
Bury St Edmunds, Suffolk IP32 6BB
t: (+44) 01284 700321
www.arimapublishing.com

DEDICATION

To our Grandchildren

Ebibrabowei, Osagioduwa, Chinemelum & others.

CONTENTS

PREFACE

If a person wants to start a business, the very first hurdle he will need to contend with is the decision on what type of business to undertake.

Business Management is an encompassing book designed to meet the fundamental cravings of business students, teachers, managers, employees, entrepreneurs and others, for knowledge on management theories, techniques for effective communication, human resource development and interpersonal relationship.

In this era of globalization and technological sophistication and innovations, efficient and effective business management have posed a serious challenge to entrepreneurs, managers, educationists and other related professionals.

This book, therefore, presents the basics of theory and practice of business management, it is encompassing as it covers all necessary facets for the practitioners of business management, from feasibility study, management theories, banking, personnel management to computer basics. The role of effective communication cannot be over-emphasized as it is a sine-qua-non in ensuring that all concerned personnel are aware of the set goals of the organization.

Furtherance, there are constant interactions between the business organization and its numerous environments that require harmonious resolutions.

The concept, theories, principles and techniques highlighted in this book are to enable the business managers and personnel develop skills that will assist them in realizing their goals. However, there are no universal acceptance of a "best way", the manager should apply the most suitable option based on the realities of specific situations.

I hereby acknowledge and appreciate the contributions of numerous colleagues and assistants. The challenges from students and professionalism are also contributory to the realization of this work: and most importantly, thanks to you my readers.

CHAPTER 1

ESTABLISHING A BUSINESS

If a person wants to start a business, the very first hurdle he will need to contend with is the decision on what type of business to undertake.

Having scaled the first hurdle, the next one is to carry out a thorough investigation on the feasibility or viability of such a business venture. This feasibility study is to enable the prospective businessman to be aware of the requirements of such a business, that is, the dos and don'ts. This study can be carried out by the prospective businessman or he can employ the services of a professional consultant who is knowledgeable about the type of business.

It is very necessary and important to conduct a feasibility study because the findings therefrom will enable the prospective businessman to make a final decision whether or not he should still engage in the business.

One often wonders why some businessmen dabble into one line of business to another, or soon get bankrupt. A simple explanation is that they did not have an organized planning system and so carried out their businesses in haphazard manner.

The feasibility report will, therefore, highlight both short and long-term benefits and constraints. It presents a comprehensive analysis of future trends, management

1

requirements and flexibility to ensure ease to changes in both internal and external environments.

Basically, the report should provide information on the following areas.

1. **Finance**

All the expected activities of the business must be expressed in quantitative terms, from registration of the business, location, materials, equipment to personnel requirements. This aspect of the report is the most important because all other activities and success of the business will hinge on it.

The financial analyses will highlight:

a. Availability of short and long- term funds, the initial capital requirement, prospects of future borrowing, sources of borrowing, estimated interest rate and other conditions of borrowing.

b. Cash flow analyses of sales, overhead expenditure and profit margin.

c. Accounting ratios and projections should be prepared to enable the prospective businessman anticipate his business stand, especially working capital.

2. **Product/Service**

The relevance of the product/ service to the market, the composition and benefits derivable by the consumers should be analyzed. Price elasticity determination, demand and the life cycle should also be projected.

If it is a manufacturing outfit, then the sources of raw materials and availability both in quantity and quality should be indicated. Stocks, warehousing cost and stock control technicalities should be stated. If the venture is to deal on finished goods, the suppliers, quantity, quality and cost should be projected.

3. **Marketing**

    a. The potential target market should be identified and to ensure that the goods or services to be provided conform to what potential customers want. It should also anticipate and supply goods to customers' requirements efficiently and effectively.

    b. Marketing strategies to be employed to ensure effective promotional mix. The types of promotion, budget and stages of the product life cycle.

    c. Distributive channels to be utilized in ensuring that products get to the target market.

    d. The feasibility report should analyze the sales turnover rate projection and profit level.

    e. Competitors or close substitutes to the intended business should be taken cognizance of.

    f. Research, pricing technique, after- sales services, credit granting policy, branding and packaging, all these need to be highlighted in order to guide the potential investor on making proper business decision.

4.   Personnel

The human resource is the most crucial aspect of a business. An organization can have all the modern, sophisticated equipment or machineries, but man will be required to operate them. Hence, the feasibility report should indicate the calibre of workers that will be needed whether skilled, semi- skilled or unskilled.

a.   The manpower needs, the number and quality, training needs and cost, organizational structure, responsibilities and authority, job descriptions and specifications should be indicated.

b.   Conditions of service and remunerations to different cadre or category of personnel should also be projected.

c.   The Management team also needs to be known, that is, the number and calibre of people that will be required to direct the affairs of the business.

5.   Location

The most appropriate location for the business should be indicated, this is very important if the balance of cost factors and profitability is to be taken into consideration.

The main focus of a business is to maximize profit, minimize cost while satisfying customers, hence, cost factors to be noted should include availability of infrastructure, such as, accessible roads, rails, airport, effective communication system, light and water which are crucial for success in business. Others include nearness to raw materials/ goods, labour, market, financial institutions and other servicing outfits, adequate information should be provided to indicate the situation of such conveniences.

In summary, feasibility study entails a thorough investigation of the business environment that will provide strategic situational information about the past, present and future prospect of an intending business, it should also analyze the strengths, weaknesses, opportunities and threats (SWOT) associated with such business venture. The information thus obtained will reveal the economic viability of the line of business for the specific environment and circumstances, the financial requirement, raw materials or stock sources, government policies, machineries required, cultural, social and religious biases, personnel requirement in terms of number and qualifications, the market situation in terms of sales, competition and profitability. Such information obtained will be collated, sorted and analyzed and a report will be produced and studied critically, after which the potential businessman will decide if the business is worth investing in or not.

Problems of Feasibility Report by Consultants

1. Feasibility studies are often not conducted by experts. There is yet no professional body to regulate the activities of the Consultants, hence, all comers in search of occupation claim to be business consultants.
2. Reliable advice is often not given to clients.

3.   Some feasibility reports contain serious errors, defects, inaccuracies and outright falsifications of data usually to influence financiers who will be misled into granting financial advances based on such reports.

4.   Some consultants have already prepared reports on popular business proposals and are often given to clients without taking cognizance of the specific locations and circumstances of such clients.

5.   Some clients, probably because of financial constraints, tend to patronize consultants from whom the fees are low and thereby get inefficient services. Similarly, some consultants charge ridiculously high fees that scare clients from them.

CHAPTER 2

BUSINESS ORGANIZATION

Probably the most influential book in the entire field of management is the classic treatise entitled: **The Functions of the Executive** by Chester I. Barnard in 1938 (Harvard University Press) which was geared towards maintaining a system of cooperative effort in a formal **organization.**

The logical steps postulated by him are that:

1. Physical, biological psychological, and social limitations of individuals lead them to cooperate, to work in group, to be interdependent since one tree cannot make a forest or a man an island.

2. The act of cooperation leads to the establishment of cooperative systems in which physical, biological, personal and social factors or elements are present, and that the continuation of cooperation depends on effectiveness and efficiency.

3. Cooperative system may be divided into "organization" and "other elements". The organization involves the interaction of people in the system, while other elements could be the environments, political, economic, social and finance.

4. Organization can also be classified as formal and informal. Formal organization is that set of consciously,

coordinated social interactions that has deliberate and joint purposes, while informal is a loose association.

Among others, in formal organization the people involved must be able to communicate with one another, contribute to group action, and have a conscious common purpose.

It should have a leader whose responsibility it is to integrate the whole and find the best balance between conflicting forces and events.

Organization is a loosely used word with many management theorists, some would say, it includes all the behaviour of all participants, others equate it with the total system of social and cultural relationships, - the act of organizing or the process of being organized comprising of elements with varied responsibilities or functions that contribute to the whole and to collective purpose or attainment of set goals. Examples include, business firms, political parties, religious, educational, cultural and social association, government offices and hospitals.

However, in the business management context, **Organization** means defining or setting clear-cut tasks that must be completed in order to achieve corporate aims and objectives. These are achieved by grouping the work into logical areas with adequate, appropriate personnel and allocating authority and responsibility to carry out those tasks.

In general terms, organizations exist because they can achieve results which individuals cannot achieve alone. By coming together, individuals overcome limitations imposed by physical environment, biological, psychological and social limitations. Chester I. Barnard (1956) used the example of a man trying to move a stone that was too large for him.

The big stone = environmental factor.

The size of the man = biological factor, but after forming an organization with another man, they both moved the stone with combined efforts.

However, Brown (1960) observed that some of the concern about the restrictive dangers of informal organization arise from poor organizational practices. There should be room for use of discretion of workers, for taking advantage of creative talents.

Types of Business Organization

There are basically three types of business organization:

(a)   The sole proprietorship (business undertakings conducted by individuals)

(b)   Partnership (by two or more persons)

(c)   By companies (through sale of shares by private or public limited businesses)

But there are other types such as:

(d)   Holding companies

(e)   Public boards and corporations

(f)   Local governments

(g)   Associations of persons in societies such as building and co-operative societies and

(h)   Trade associations.

Some of these forms of business organizations can be applied to a variety of undertakings as in the company form, while others, such as cooperative societies are specialized types created to suit particular circumstances or businesses.

Only in the case of the sole trader and the partnership do the proprietors directly own the business. In other forms, an artificial body regarded in law as a separate person or legal entity owns the business and has perpetual succession, in the sense that it continues in existence regardless of changes by reason of deaths and other causes amongst the members or founders. The artificial person so created is termed **Corporation,** which can sue and be sued.

These various types of business organizations differ from each other according to:

(a) The ownership of the business

(b) The formation requirements

(c) Sources of capital

(d) The amount of capital invested

(e) The composition of controller(s)

(f) The accountability of the controller(s)

(g) The division of the profits

(h) The degree of liability

(i) Continuity of existence

(a) **The Ownership of the Business**

The ownership of the businesses could be classified as public or private.

The public ones are owned by Federal, State or Local Governments which include ministries, parastatals, courts, hospital, schools and public corporations which provide electricity, water, transportation and other highly subsidized goods like petroleum products.

The private ownership comprises of Joint Stock Companies (Public or Private), partnership and sole proprietorship. The companies are owned by their shareholders, two or more individuals own the partnership firm while a single individual owns a sole proprietorship

(b)   The Formation Requirement

Any seven or more persons can form a public company (two or more for private company) subscribing to a Memorandum and Articles of Association, attaching and filing, all relevant documents, paying necessary fees and register with the Registrar of Companies. Companies can also be formed by special Act of Parliament or Decree. Partnership firm can be formed by two to twenty individuals with the firm registered and "Partnership Agreement" drawn up, explicitly specifying the rights, duties, privileges and obligations of partners.

The sole proprietor has no such complex legal formalities.

(c)   Sources of Capital

Companies have assess to numerous sources to raise their capital such as bank loans, overdrafts, trade credit, debentures, and shares, Government agencies use foreign loans, bonds, fines, levics, and taxes.

The partners pool their resources together as capital, while the sole proprietor depends solely on his savings and money borrowed from friends and relations.

(d)   **The Amount of Capital Invested**

This varies from business to business. The amount of capital employed will depend largely on the type of business in terms of size, products or services, location, management, labour and machineries. However, government and multinational companies will be more capital intensive than partnership or sole-proprietorship.

(e)   **The Composition of Controller(s)**

Most companies are controlled by board of directors or management board.

The partners control the partnership, while the sole –proprietor controls his business.

(f)   **The Accountability of the Controller(s)**

The controllers of companies or government departments and organization must be accountable to their owners.

The partners are accountable to themselves and the sole- proprietor is accountable to no one but himself.

(g)   **The Division of Profits**

Companies retain most of their profits for re-investment or ploughed back into the business; some, in addition, pay out part of their profits as dividends or profit shares to their shareholders. In some cases, part of the profit might be paid to the organization's employees as part of an incentive scheme.

The government ploughs back whatever profit is made into areas of need in the economy.

The partners share their profits according to the agreed percentage or ratio as contained in their partnership agreement.

The sole proprietor owns all the business profits.

(h)   **The Degree of Liability**

In companies, the liability of shareholders is limited to the value of the shares held. That is, the shareholders are not required to contribute any additional amount to off set the companies liabilities.

The partnership and sole- proprietorship, however, have unlimited liability for the debts of the business. That is, if the business assets are not enough to pay creditors, the personal assets of such partners or sole –proprietor may be used to settle the debts.

(i)   **Continuity of Existence**

As a legal entity, the continuous existence of a company is not affected by even the death of the largest shareholder.

But the death of a partner or, sole proprietor may terminate the business.

Sole-Proprietorship

A sole-proprietorship is a business concern owned by an individual. He provided the Capital, with which the business was started, employs the necessary labour or runs it alone. He, directs the business, makes decisions about the methods and amount of trade.

The sole-proprietor takes all the profits and bears the losses alone. He has flexible working hours and shows greater personal interest in the business.

The sole-proprietorship, mainly in the retail trade, is the dominant type of trade in most societies.

The Advantages of Sole-Proprietorship

The main advantages of the sole-proprietorship are as follows:

(a) *Ease of entry:* There are no formal procedures required to enter the business except in certain types of business in which licences may be obtained or fees paid.

(b) *Decision-making:* The decision- making is usually swift as the sole proprietor is under no obligation to consult with anyone else. The success of his business largely depends on the type of decisions he makes.

(c) *Customer Service:* The sole–proprietorship has immensurable personal interest in the business. He has close personal contact with his customers and strives to satisfy them. He renders efficient services, grants credit sales to reliable customers, can transport the goods to customer's destination, and other personalized services.

(d) *Flexibility:* He can operate flexible working hours in order to satisfy his customers. He can also change his line of commodities or services in tune with current taste, fashion or economic trend.

14

(e)   *Privacy:* The sole–proprietor enjoys a very high degree of privacy in his business, he is under no obligation to reveal the state of his finances to anyone except for tax purposes. He also has his trade secrets, so long as they are legitimate.

(f)   *Distribution of Profits:* The sole proprietor gains all the profits. He does not distribute or share the profits with anyone else. He is to solely enjoy the fruits of his labour.

(g)   *Dissolution:*   The sole–proprietor does not need any formalities to wind – up his business. Easy entry, easy exit.

The Disadvantages of Sole-Proprietorship

The disadvantages of sole proprietorship are:

(a)   *Unlimited Liability:* The owner's liabilities are unlimited, that means that he is personally liable for all the debts of the business even to the extent of forfeiting his personal assets. In situations where he is insolvent, he can be sued and can earn jail term or declared bankrupt. This means that the sole- proprietorship is a high risk venture.

(b)   *Inadequate Capital:* A single proprietor has only a limited capital which could make business expansion difficult. He will also not be able to benefit from bulk purchase, or employ experts to assist him. He may also not have collateral to enable him secure loan from finance houses.

(c)   *Continuity:* The death of the sole-proprictor often leads to the termination of the business. The next-of-kin may

15

not have grasped the business technique or may not be willing to continue with the business.

(d)   *Long Working Hours:* Since the success of the business solely rest on the efforts of the sole-proprietor; he tends to work for long hours. He also works at awkward hours, weekends, public holidays and rarely has time for rest or vacation. If he is sick or decides to take a vacation, the business will suffer and he might even loose some of his customers to business rivals.

(e)   *Employee Turnover:* In situations where the sole-proprietor employs workers, it is evident that there is high turnover rate. The workers do not work for long and tend to seek greener pastures because there may be no tenure or prospects of ever sharing in the management or profit.

Partnership

Partnership is defined as the relationship which exists between persons carrying on business in common with a view of making profit.

Two to twenty people can carry on business as partners, they provide the capital and share the responsibilities for the business, on an agreed bases.

Every partner is an agent of the firm and his other partners for the purpose of the business of the partnership. He has implied power to buy, sell or pledge goods, ordinarily dealt in by the firm, to make and endorse promissory notes, bills of exchange, cheques, open an account and borrow money on behalf of the firm.

Partners are bound to render true accounts and full information to other partners, any profit made must be disclosed and surrendered.

Property brought into the business by the partners or subsequently acquired by the firm is partnership property and, therefore, jointly owned by all the partners.

The persons who have agreed to carry on business together are jointly called "the firm".

To prevent difference or litigations arising in the future, an agreement is usually drawn up and signed by the partners.

This agreement is called the **Partnership Deed** or the **Articles of Partnership** and contains information such as:

1. The firm's name, the nature of the business to be carried on and the address or addresses at which business is to be transacted.

2. The agreed capital, in cash and/or kind, to be brought into the firm by each partner.

3. The proportion in which the profits and losses of the firm are to be shared.

4. Whether interest should be paid on capital contributed and at what rate.

5. The life-span of the partnership.

6. Whether interest should be paid on drawings and at what rate

7. Whether partners working full- time in the firm are entitled to salaries and the agreed salaries.

8. The interest to be paid to a partner who loans money to the firm.

9. The necessary accounting books should be properly kept and audited. All partners should have access to

them. Agreed periodic financial statements should also be stated.

10.   Circumstances in which the partnership can be dissolved.

11.   Circumstances in which new partners(s) can be admitted.

12.   What should be done when a partner retires, dies or is seriously ill.

Types of Partners

1.   *Ordinary (or Active) Partner:*
     This is a partner that has invested capital in the firm and takes an active part in the running of the business.

2.   *Sleeping (or Dormant) Partner:*
     This is a partner who has invested capital in the firm but does not take part in the conduct of the business. He is faceless and his name may not even appear in the firm's name. However, he is very much liable for the debts of the firm.

3.   *Nominal (or Apparent or Quasi or Ostensible) Partner:*
     This person is really not a partner, he has not contributed any capital but he has allowed his name to be used in the business, such a person is said to be "holding out" as a partner. He is, however, liable for the debts of the firm on the assumption that he is a partner.
     An example of this is a retired partner who left his capital in the form of a loan on which he earns interest. His name is still been used in the business but he is no longer a partner.

18

The Advantages of Partnership

1. It is easy to form no formal procedure is required except to draw up the Deed of Partnership.
2. There is privacy in the affairs of the business, partners can keep information as to trading profits and liabilities, to themselves.
3. Additional finance may be brought into the partnership, permitting the business to expand more rapidly than is possible with a sole trader.
4. The responsibilities of running the business can now be shared thus making it possible for partners to enjoy reduced working hours, have holidays and less worry in case of ill health.
5. By division of responsibilities some degree of specialization is made possible Wider skills and experience are brought to the firm which, when combined offer a more comprehensive service to the consumer.
6. Two good heads are better than one, with the need for partners to consult among themselves before decisions are made; they are, therefore, better placed to make wiser decisions.
7. In the event of insolvency, the burden rests on all the partners, that is, the risk of the business is now shared among partners, rather than been borne by one person.
8. It is flexible and adjustment to change can be swiftly or promptly done, this is possible because of the personal interest of the partners

The Disadvantages of Partnership

1. The liabilities of the partnership are unlimited.
2. Decision making process is slow since partners must consult one another before committing the partnership.
3. The independence or privacy hitherto enjoyed by a sole proprietor is lost. He now has to share everything with other partners, especially the profits.
4. The partnership is adversely affected by the death, retirement, ill-health or bankruptcy of a partner, as the partnership might be dissolved.
5. Difficulties may result where a partner, acting with implied authority, binds other partners in an unprofitable deal or one that will task them both physically and financially.
6. Capital available may be adversely affected by a partner's death, when his share in the business is used to pay his beneficiaries.

Dissolution of Partnership

The Articles of Partnership should contain circumstances under which a partnership can be dissolved. Among these are, that a partnership can be dissolved.

1. By the expiration of an agreed period of the partnership if entered into for a fixed period.
2. By the completion or termination of an agreed business undertaking if the partnership was formed for that venture
3. By any partner giving notice of dissolution to the other partner(s)
4. By the death or bankruptcy of any partner.

5. By court ruling or any unlawful act by the firm which makes its continuous existence impossible. The court can decree a dissolution in cases where a partner is insane, sick or has persistently broken the terms of the agreement or has been guilty of a criminal offence or misconduct.

The court can also order a dissolution of a firm if the firm is continuously run at a loss.

Upon dissolution of the partnership, the property of the partnership is applied in payment of external liabilities of the firm, then partners' loans to the firm and payments of what may be due to the partners respectively.

In the case of bankruptcy, the partnership property is referred to as **joint estate** while the private properties of the partners are referred to as **separate estates**.

The funds realized from the sale of the joint estate are applied as follows:

1. To pay external creditors, that is, partnership debts.
2. The proceeds from the sale of the separate estates are applied first to pay debts of the individual partners.
3. Any surplus from the joint estate is distributed amongst the partners in the ratio of their respective capital.
4. Any surplus from the separate estate is shared amongst the partners according to their agreed proportion in which they shared profit.

Limited Liability Companies

Limited Liability Company, also called, Joint Stock Company, consists of a number of persons united for the purpose of carrying on a business and incorporated by the company's Act or Decree in force.

It is a legal entity capable of holding property, acquiring rights and incurring obligations, suing or being sued, and having perpetual succession.

Companies may be divided into three classes
(a)   Companies limited by shares
(b)   Companies limited by guarantee and
(c)   Unlimited companies.

Unlimited companies are rare; companies limited by guarantee are usually of a philanthropic or non-trading nature.

All trading companies are limited by shares, where a company is limited by shares, the share capital is divided into shares of a fixed amount and each member's liability is limited to the amount, if any, unpaid on his shares. Shareholders who have fully paid cannot be called upon to pay anything further towards the company's liability.

Companies may be further classified as public and private.

Registration of Limited Liability Companies

The responsibility for the registration of Limited Liability Companies (Joint Stock Companies), hitherto, laid with the Registrar of Companies, Federal Ministry of Commerce and Industry. But with the promulgation of the Companies and Allied Matters Decree (CAMD) No. 1 of 1990, this function was transferred to the newly established Corporate Affairs Commission (CAC). The mandate of the CAC included the regulation and supervision of the formation, incorporation, management and winding-up of companies. The CAC was also saddled with the responsibilities for the registration and management of business names, converting a private company to a public one; allotment of shares; registration of mortgages, debentures and charges; changes of company name, objects, directors, secretaries and registered office/head office address.

Furthermore, the CAC is to ensure that annual returns are filed every year by directors of companies or bi-annual in the case of financial houses, such as banks, insurance, deposit and provident. It may also appoint one or more competent inspectors to investigate the affairs of a company whenever the need arises. It is also the responsibility of the CAC to effect merger or amalgamation of companies; winding up voluntarily or by the courts.

Memorandum of Association

This document governs the relationship of the company with the external world. Its seven main clauses are:

1. The name of the company with the word **limited** as the last word, or Plc. This is to warn people who will do business with such company that the shareholders have limited liability.

2. The address of the company's headquarter.

3. The objects of the company. This states what the company will do when it is established. This will form the legal basis for its activities, shareholders can sue and even withdraw their investments if the directors deviate from their legal registered activities.

4. A statement that the liability of the members is limited.

5. The amount of share capital to be issued, and the types of share.

6. An undertaking by the signatories that they do desire to be registered as a company and to pay for the shares against their names.

7. The names of the directors and secretary should be stated.

Articles of Association

This document controls the internal affairs of the company, such as, how meetings, are to be conducted, the duties, responsibilities and authorities of officers.

Certificate of Incorporation

To obtain a certificate of incorporation, that is, the legal document authorizing the promoters to commence business, the promoters must present the following to the Registrar of Companies.

1. The memorandum of Association
2. The articles of Association
3. The statement of the nominal capital
4. A statutory declaration that the Company's Act Regulations have been complied with. Then the Registrar will issue a Certificate of Incorporation, which makes the company a separate legal personality. The company can now commence business and operate within the legal basis of its activities. It can own land and other properties, employ people, sue and be sued in court.

The private company will raise its capital from contributions of members, while the public company will need to obtain its capital from the public either directly and / or indirectly through institutional investors or financial houses.

Certificate of Trading

The issuance of the Certificate of Trading concludes the registration of company process.

It is obtained after the promoters have deposited the following documents with the Registrar of Companies.

(a)   A statement that the minimum capital has been subscribed.

(b)   A statement that the directors have paid for their shares

(c)   A statutory declaration that the Companies Acts have been complied with.

The minimum capital is the least amount required for the successful take–off of the company. If this minimum capital is not obtained, all the capital collected must be returned to the subscribers.

Similarities

Features common to both Public and Private Limited Liability Companies.

1.   Incorporated both types of company assume separate legal existence from the owners (the shareholders). They both have rights and privileges as human beings to own property, sue and be sued in court.

2.   They both enjoy limited liability. The liability of their members are limited only to the amount of capital contributed by them and will not be required to

contribute any amount further in the case of liquidation of the company.

3. Both companies raise capital through the sale of shares.

4. Both companies have to comply with the requirements of the Company's Acts and Decree to secure incorporation.

5. They both distribute profit to shareholders in the form of dividend.

6. The shareholders of both companies delegate the managing function to a group of persons known collectively as the Board of Directors of the Companies.

7. Both companies must file statutory returns with the Registrar of Companies/ Corporate Affairs Commission annually.

8. They are both private enterprises and are profit oriented.

9. Both have continuity of existence.

Dissimilarities

	Public	Private
1.	Can transfer shares freely at the Stock Exchange Market.	Restricts the right to transfer shares except with the consent of other members.
2.	No limit to membership except when shares are all subscribed for.	Limits the number of its members, excluding employees, to fifty.

3.	Invites the public to subscribe for its shares.	Prohibits any invitation to the public to subscribe for its shares or debentures.
4.	Usually minimum of seven, but at times two, persons may form a public company by subscribing to a Memorandum of Association and filing it with certain other documents prescribed by the Act and by the payment of the requisite duty and fees.	Minimum number is two.
5.	Annual report must be published for public consumption.	There is privacy, does not publish its Financial statement.

Co-operative Societies

This is a form of business organization which brings a group of individuals together to carry on business for the benefit of themselves.

There are laws regulating the activities of cooperative societies, these vary from state to state, but generally, there are very few variations.

The group members must be at least ten, each of whom must be qualified to be a member of the type of cooperative society for which they are seeking registration.

The cooperative society must give its operative address and three copies of its proposed bye-laws to the Registrar of Co-operative societies.

On the death of a member, his shares are transferred to his named beneficiary.

There must be a register containing all the name of the members and date of membership.

Each member has a voting right, no matter the amount invested in the society. However, no one member can own more that one- fifth of the society's capital.

Co-operative societies can also invest in viable projects with the approval of the registrar of co-operative societies. He should also be consulted for the disposal of surplus income for payment of dividend or bonuses and the society must keep at least one- quarter of its net surplus incomes in a reserve fund.

Types of Cooperative Societies

1. *Agricultural produce marketing/farmers multi purpose societies*: They engage in the producing and marketing of agricultural products especially export products.

2. *Consumers Cooperative Societies:* They engage in bulk buying and retailing of consumer goods to members.

3. *Cooperative loans and thrift societies:* They encourage thrift and saving habits by collecting subscriptions from members. They help members to set up petty trade and handicraft industries.

4. *Cooperative Craftsmen' Societies*: These are associations of people of the same trade who contribute to obtain raw materials to work together.

5. *Cooperative wholesales societies:* They engage in bulk buying and selling to the public.

6. *Cooperative Housing/Building Societies:* They help members to own their houses.

7. *Producers' Cooperative Society:* Formed by manufacturers who come together to have a clear-cut policy as regards the purchase of raw- materials or other factors of production and the distribution among themselves.

Advantages of Cooperative Societies

1. They are democratically managed, that is, one-man one vote irrespective of the number of shares owned.

2. Consumers are protected from constant fluctuation in prices.

3. They sell at a cheaper rate to members.

4. Members can pull their resources together to start a big business.

5. They encourage thrift by providing facilities for savings.

6. They assist members in marketing their products and reduce exploitation by middlemen.

7. They are able to raise loans through cooperative and savings banks.

8. They provide assistance in the education of their members' families.

9. They buy goods in bulk at control prices.

Problems Facing Cooperative Societies

1. The managers are usually part-time elected members and therefore, do not put in their best in the organization of the enterprise.
2. They do not have enough money to employ experts.
3. They lack sufficient initial capital as they depend on small subscriptions from members who are usually not rich people.
4. Some members do not have formal education and as such they are not actively committed.
5. The problem of bad debts also exists when some members find it difficult to repay loans granted them.
6. There is the problem of misappropriation of funds by the officials.

Holding Companies

A holding company is one that has acquired control of another company by the purchases of a t least 51 percent of its voting shares. The holding company is then regarded as the parent company and can gradually build up a large-scale business.

By owning at least 51% of the voting shares control can be secured and the subsidiary company brought within the direct influence of the parent company.

The small company will benefit from the parent company's research, technical know- how, marketing and welfare economies, while the parent company will enjoy regular supply of raw materials, transport, component, supply, marketing, advertising and research fields.

Share Capital

The amount required by a company is usually stated in the Memorandum of Association. The amount required will depend on the type of business proposed. A share is a part of the total amount of capital, that is, the capital sum, divided into fixed amount. For instance, if ten million naira is required as capital, a share could be worth 25 kobo, 50 kobo or ₦1.

The capital approved by the Registrar of the Corporate Affairs Commission is usually referred to as the Nominal, Authorized or Registered Capital. The 50 kobo share is most commonly used now. The incorporated company will then advertise and appeal to the public to contribute to its capital by buying stocks of its shares. This is, however, for only Public Limited Companies (Plc) not applicable to private ones.

The 50 kobo, for instance, is referred to as the par value or face value and subscribers apply for numbers that they can afford, and when allocated, they become shareholders of the company.

Shares can be sold at par value, discount or premium. In recent times, shares are hardly issued at par value; rather, they are issued at a premium. Premium shares are those issued above par value, for example, a 50 kobo share issued at ₦1.85, the difference of ₦1.35 is the premium. On the other hand, shares issued at a discount, which is very rare now, are those selling below the par value, that is, a 50 kobo share being issued for 43 kobo, the difference of 7 kobo is the discount.

There is no limit to the number of shareholders a public company may have except that it does not exceed its authorized share capital.

The classes of shares are presented in the table below.

Classes of Shares

Type of Investment	Reward earned	Degree of	Who issue them
Ordinary Shares	equal share of profits: hence nickname' equity shares'	risk carry the main risk	Private and Public Companies
Deferred Ordinary Shares, (Founder's Shares).	Share of profits after ordinary shares have had some (say 10%) profit.	Same as Ordinary Shares	Public Companies
Preference Shares.	Definite rate of dividend (say 7%), but only if profits are made.	Less than Ordinary Share as they usually Have a prior right to repayment.	Pubic and Private Companies.
Cumulative Preference Share	As above, but if profits are not earned in one year the dividend accumulates and is not lost.	As above	As above
Participating Preference Shares	After taking the fixed rate (say 7%) these shares earn extra dividend if the Ordinary Shares get more than 7%.	As above	As above

Debentures (loans to companies; debentures are not really shares)	Payable whether profits are Fixed Rate of interest (say 6%). made or not.	Very small	Public and Private Companies, if permitted by their Articles.

Shares can also be over-subscribed or under-subscribed. If the issue was for 31,419,000 ordinary shares of 50k each at ₦3.50k per share; but if 40,000,000 shares were applied for, then the issue is said to be over-subscribed. But, it will be under-subscribed, if the applications received amounted to only 25,000,220 shares.

In the case of over-subscription, the authorized capital cannot be exceeded; hence, applications are adjusted on pro rata. If full payment accompanied applications, then refunds will be made to affected applicants.

The first outing for a public company in the Stock Exchange Market and advertised for the public to subscribe for are referred to as the Initial Public Offer (IPO) also, for a hitherto private Limited Liability Company, becoming a public company.

Dividends

When companies make profit and decide to declare it for its shareholders, the sharing of this portion of the profit is referred to as the dividends. Every shareholder will get his share of the profit according to the number of shares owned. For instance, if 2kobo per share dividend is declared, the shareholders will multiply their share holdings by 2kobo to determine their amount of profit. This will also depend on the classes of shares owned by the shareholders. Dividends can also be in form of shares, that is, a shareholder maybe given an additional share for every one share owned or at times in both cash and shares.

Dividend warrants: These are cheques issued to shareholders by the company for the payment of their dividends.

Unclaimed Dividends

This situation arises when dividend warrants are not claimed by some shareholders. This has become worrisome to the Federal Government of recent. To protect the interest of the shareholders, the period for equity holders to claim their dividends have been increased from six to twelve years, before they can be declared unclaimed.

Reasons adduced for unclaimed dividends are:

1. Some shareholders do not operate current bank account and so may not be able to deposit and cash their dividend warrants.

2. Information about deceased shareholders may not be known to the company and no next of kin indicated.

3. Where a bank is not easily located near shareholder's residence, he may decide that the amount to be claimed is too small to worry about, if it will cost more in terms of transportation, to claim it.

4. Shareholders do not often inform the company of change of address and so dividend warrants are returned to the company.

5. Dividend warrants could also be lost on transit.

6. Some shareholders could have received the warrant but failed to cash it or have misplaced it.
7. Unclaimed dividend warrants register are usually not published by some companies to enable affected public to react.
8. Shareholders also need to be enlightened and advised on how to claim their dividends.
9. Some Registrars of Companies could deliberately not update their shareholders records so as to retain the unclaimed money in their companies.
10. The colossal number of shareholders of some companies could lead to inefficiency on the part of officers in-charge of compiling, writing and dispatching dividend warrants to shareholders.
11. Dividend warrants are cheques and so become stale after six months of issue. Shareholders have to return such warrants to the company for renewal and most do not want to go through such trouble.

Offer by Way of Rights

This occurs when a public limited company decides to raise more capital by issuance of shares. Offer by way of rights is, therefore, a privilege offer to only existing shareholders to subscribe for the available shares offered. The amount per share by way of rights is usually lower than that of new subscribers.

Debentures

Situations may arise when a company will require additional funds to finance a project or take advantage of business opportunities. The company may source for loans from banks, individuals or other financial houses, but if these are not successful, especially if it is to be a long-term loan, it might decide to issue debentures. Debentures are similar to shares, but are not shares, debenture holders do not own a part of the company, but rather, they are creditors. Debenture holders loan money to the company and are given a document called a debenture, which contains amount of money borrowed, interest rate, and terms of repayment. There are fixed and floating debentures, fixed debentures are attached to specific projects, such as mortgage and if there is default in meeting the terms of agreement, such assets could be claimed to reimburse the debenture holders. On the other hand, floating debentures are not tied to any specific asset. Debenture, therefore, is a loan to the company and interest must be paid whether the company makes a profit or not.

CHAPTER 3

BUSINESS ENVIRONMENTS

The success of a business is largely dependent on the degree of interaction with is environments. A business does not operate in isolation; it has to consider all the forces that can affect its continued existence.

The environments within which the business operates include the following:

1. Laws and regulations
2. Political
3. Economic
4. Social/cultural/ethical/religions
5. Technological
6. Physical
7. Demographic
8. Customers
9. Suppliers
10. Competitors
11. Investors and owners
12. Local community
13. General public
14. Management

Figure 1 Current Environments of Business

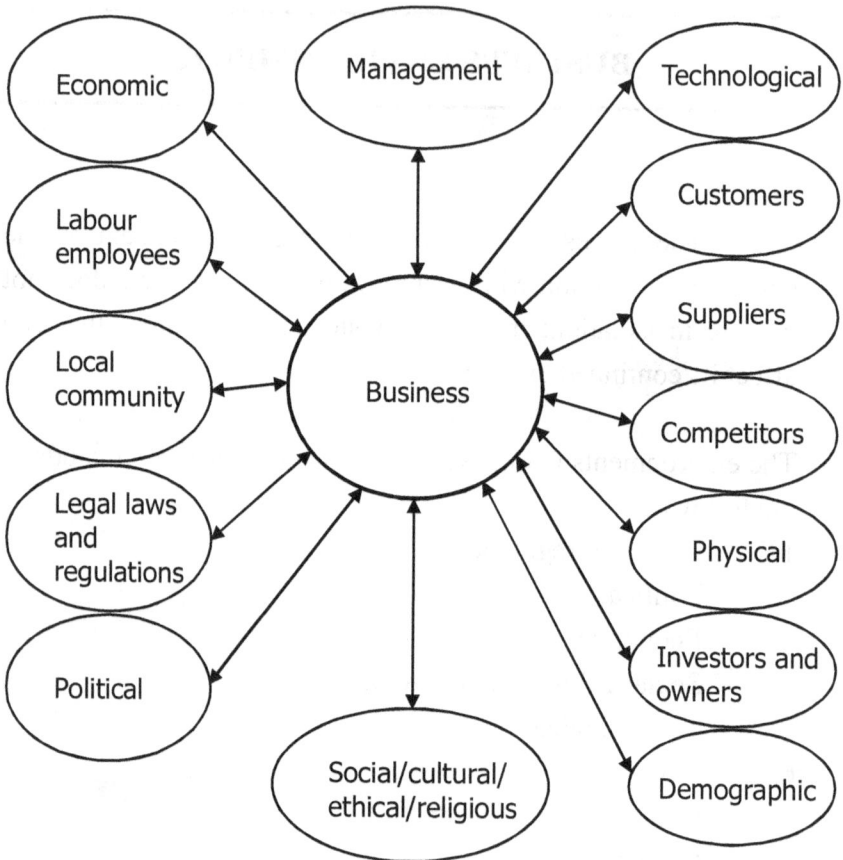

1. **Legal Environment**

   This constitutes all the laws or decrees or edicts made by the governments in Nigeria that is, Federal, State and Local Governments, to regulate business operations. Such laws include the Company's Act, the Food and Drug Act, the Enterprise Promotion Decree, and others.

A business is required to operate within the laws and regulations of the country or face prosecution or closure. These laws define the legal environment and are sometimes regulatory or restrictive and sometimes facilitating, that is, giving assistance to the establishments of new businesses or incentives to existing ones.

2.   Political Environment

This refers to the system of government existing and the administrative subdivisions of the country which affect business operations. Government play a multiple role in business in Nigeria, first by owning fully business enterprises, by owning considerable proportion of the shares in several other companies and by being the single largest institutional consumer.

The political atmosphere in a country will influence the nature of laws and regulations, will also determine the operations of businesses as they are bound to adapt to changing political situations.

The more democratic and stable a government is the better the political environment for businesses because political instability adversely affects business operations.

3.   Economic Environment

Nigeria, today, is characterized as a developing country with low income per capital, low technological know how low, level of legacy, inadequate infrastructure such as roads, electricity, water, health and communication system.

The country is heavily populated and dependent on the oil sector to provide a large percentage of her resources.

The economic environment of a country, therefore, includes the general economic conditions which affect business decisions such as economic growth, or boom, recession and inflation.

It also includes the government's fiscal and monetary policies with which government stimulates and controls economic activities.

A wise businessman should, thus, be very knowledgeable about his environment, to observe and analyze changes in it with a view to identifying economic opportunities and threats.

Figure 2   Economic Environment

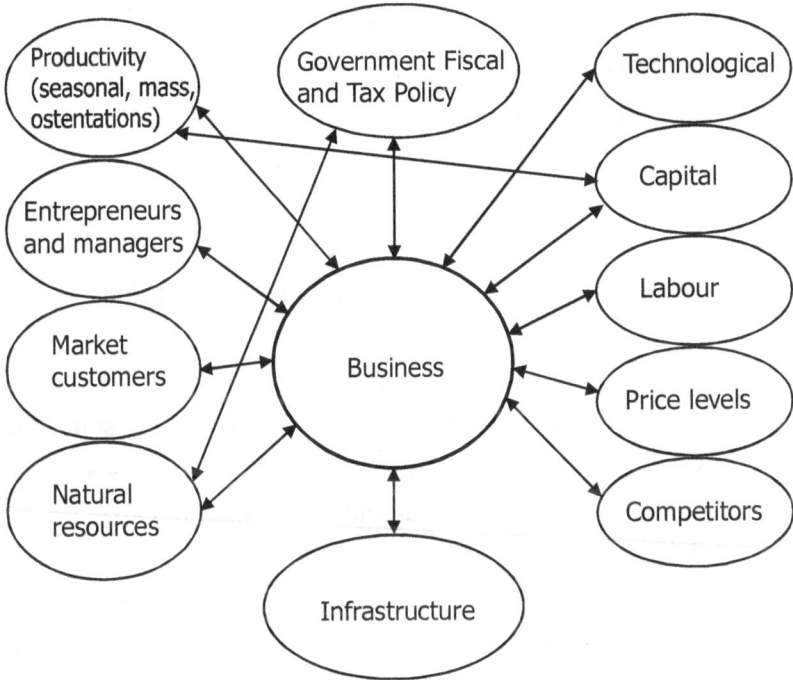

Figure 2   Economic Environment

4.   Social/Cultural/Religious/Ethical Environment

This is defined as the social institutions family, religion, history, languages, customs, beliefs, norms and value systems prevalent in a society.

When managers plan, they are expected to take into consideration the needs and desires of members of society outside the organization as well as those of his staff. The Nigerian society, especially the immediate communities, expects the business organization to assist in the provision of certain amenities such as health centers, schools, water, electricity, and good roads. It is also expected to respect the traditional institutions and

41

rulers, elders, donations for sporting and social events, granting of scholarships and the like.

The religious environment will also determine the type of products and services that a business can deal in. The promotional blend will also be affected, the type of advertising and mode of deliverance.

Social/cultural/religions and ethical environment is a very delicate and sensitive domain that a business is bound take into consideration in all its operation.

5.   **Technological Environment**

This describes the current state of scientific knowledge, production process, machines and supportive systems that enable a nation carry on its daily life.

Advances in technology such as electronics, communication gadgets and equipment, and computerization have affected the way business activities are carried out.

As the business world is a very competitive and dynamic one, any business organization that does not adapt to such changes in technology will find itself obsolete.

6.   **Physical Environment**

This includes the climatic conditions and the natural resources available to business and the physical conditions in which a company exists and operates.

It requires a firm to be involved in ecological development and pollution and natural hazards, such as, air, water, noise, flood, soil and proper management of firm's waste.

7. **Demographic Environment**

This deals with business environment which considers the population of the states, district or area within which the business operates.

The composition of the population, in terms of age, sex, race, nationality, education and occupation; which determines the market demand for the business' products, services and the supply of labour.

CHAPTER **4**

HOME TRADE

Home trade means internal trade that is, trade which is carried on within the country. The marketing and distribution of both imported and locally produced goods from Nigeria. The Federal Ministry of Trade, Industry and Commerce and its state counterpart are in charge of the development of trade in Nigeria. The various chambers of commerce in the country have their focus on the development of trade. Home trade may be wholesaler or retailer. The wholesaler is the link between the producer and the retailer. He buys and sells in large quantities and his profit depends mainly on the size of his turnover. The retailer is the link between the wholesaler and the public. He greatly facilitates the work of distribution by supplying goods where and where they are wanted and by passing them on to the public in the form and quantities required.

Home Trade

Home Trade is important to the development of national economy by;

1.   Creating employment opportunities for

Trading

Manufacturing

Auxiliary services   – Banks

–   Insurance

44

- Transport
- Commercial centres
- Warehouses
- Light, water, and communication

2. Providing Revenue to government – through Taxes (direct/indirect) such as:

Income tax

Corporation tax

Capital gains tax

Value added tax

3. Improved standard of living because of the availability of assorted goods and services to satisfy the needs of the citizens and

4. Encouraging local production of goods and services.

Wholesaler

Wholesale trade has been through a period of change, as the traditional way of marketing through wholesalers are often by-passed by industrialists who sell directly to retailers or to the consumers.

Wholesalers have also changed from their traditional role into new fields of activities by selling directly to consumer or through mail orders. It is, therefore, difficult to define or specify which activities the wholesaler performs.

Wholesaling, traditionally, involves the buying of goods in large quantities for resale; that is, selling to retailers in small quantities for resale generally below prevailing market retail price.

Producer → Wholesaler → Retailer → Consumer

The wholesalers are, therefore, referred to as middlemen since they are between the producers and the retailers.

Functions of the Wholesaler
To Producer

1.   The wholesaler buys goods in large quantities from the producer and this enables the producer to benefit from the economies of large scale operation. The producer is then relieved of the necessity of carrying large stock or dealing with numerous retailers.

2.   The wholesaler has now assumed the risks of the business by taking over the goods from the producer. These risks are:

   (a)   That the goods may now be needed or that the sales may be slow.

   (b)   That the wholesaler might be compelled to sell off the goods at a lower price than the cost price.

   (c)   That the goods might deteriorate, expire or get spoilt.

   (d)   That the goods could be stolen pilfered or misappropriated by his employees.

   (e)   That the wholesaler might experience bad debit from retailers who might not be able to pay their debits.

3.   He transports the goods from the producer's warehouses to his own warehouse from which retailers now come to buy in smaller quantities and possibly from the producer's deport to the retailer shops.

4. He sees to the storages of the goods in his warehouse in such a way that the goods will not get spoilt, stolen or damaged before they are bought by the retailers.

5. He helps to market the goods by advertising, demonstrating and displaying them strategically for sale. It often helps the producer with other duties like packaging, branding and breaking of bulk.

6. Since he buys in bulk from the producer and pays promptly, he makes cash available for the producer for further production or to carry on with his business.

7. Since he interacts with numerous retailers, he collects vital information about the market which he conveys the producers views to the retailers thereby establishing a link with the retail outlet and providing advice on the market situation to the producer.

8. He controls the quantity of goods released to the market in order to even out the flow of goods. This is the speculative function, which keeps prices steady irrespective of natural or man-made interference with supplies. For example, the manufacturer's machine may breakdown, there could be war, flooding, bad harvest of raw materials, strikes, servicing of factory machines, etc.

9. He saves the manufacturer the trouble of distributing the goods and also the costs of physical distribution. He eliminates the need for a marketing system, which would have involved warehousing space, distribution network, sales staff accounting records and debt collection.

To Retailer

1. The wholesaler breaks bulks to a reasonable size, selling in small quantities to the retailers owing to lack of the large capital the retailers cannot buy large quantities, the wholesaler, this, fills this breach by begin a source to which the retailer turns to for replenishment of his stock in small quantities at frequent intervals.

2. The wholesaler renders financial assistance to the retailer. This has the effect of increasing the working capital of the retailer as he can obtain his goods on credit and pay the wholesaler with the money received from his customers.

3. He grades, pre-packs and prices goods. This reduces the retailer's work and enables him to serve the customer quickly.

4. He displays a variety of goods from numerous manufacturers and demonstrates or displays them as necessary.

5. He delivers goods to the retailer at as when required.

6. He chooses a convenient location and opens at convenient hours.

Types of Wholesalers

(a) Traditional
  (i) Large-scale general wholesaler
  (ii) Specialist – limited goods
  (iii) Regional – serving particular area
  (iv) Local – small scale
(b) Cash and carry
(c) Retailer-protection

(d)   Cooperation wholesaler society

(e)   Mail-order

Retailing Structure

Retailing involves sales of goods to the ultimate consumer. It involves those institutions and procedures through which the final consumer obtains services and goods in exchange for money.

The general functions of the retailer are:

Functions of the Retailer

(a)   To provide a local supply of goods

(b)   To break bulk

(c)   To serve the public personally

(d)   To prepare goods for resale

(e)   To provide after-sales service

(f)   To act as a liaison between the consumer and the wholesaler

(g)   To provide information obtained from the consumer to the wholesaler for onward transmission about the market situation of the product to the manufacturer.

Consumer → Retailer → Wholesaler → Manufacturer

Types of Retail Trade

Small-scale	*Large scale*
Peddlers	Cooperating stores
Hawkers	Department
Retail-market stall holders	Multiple shops
Sole-trader shops	Chain stores
Partnership shops	Supermarkets
	Hyper markets
	Mail-order firms

Discount seller to
Privileged group
Direct selling by
Manufacturers

Advantages of Large Scale Trading Businesses

(a)   They have many branches, great turnover, get benefit of bulk purchasing and hence the limit price.

(b)   Can afford specialist buyers for each department, well trained with wide knowledge of the class of goods to be purchased and the quality.

(c)   Get advantage of specialization at all levels through division of labour.

(d)   Better organizational planning and will often devise ways of doing work quickly and economically.

(e)   Staff can be trained on special courses.

(f)   Use of modern technology of various mechanical gadgets and devices to promote efficiency.

(g)   Can easily borrow money on more favourable terms than smallscale traders.

Disadvantages

(a)   Decline in personal service to customers and employees.

(b)   More overhead costs of staff training acquisition of technological devices and maintenance of organizational structure

CHAPTER 5

FOREIGN TRADE

Foreign trade otherwise known as international trade or external trade, involves the exchange of goods and services between one country and another, one country with several others. In other words, it is trade among the various countries of the world.

Since a country that has comparative advantage of a product or service cannot utilize all that it produced, it will then need to sell the surplus to other countries and use resources derivable from such trade to acquire what it cannot produce from other countries as no one country is self-sufficient.

Why is Nigeria exporting crude oil, agricultural product and others and importing manufactured goods, highly complex goods, technology from all corners of the world especially America and Europe?

Why is Europe importing numerous agricultural products and exchange them for their manufactured output? What will be the cost if a nation is to be completely self-sufficient? How do all countries benefit from international trade?

The key to such questions above and many more, is provided by the "theory of comparative advantage", or "comparative cost", developed many years ago by David Ricardo, John Smart Mill, and other followers of Adam Smith.

Law of Comparative Advantage

David Ricardo, stockbroker and millionaire in 1817 came up with the proof that international specialization pays for a nation. This is the famous theory of comparative advantage, or, as it is sometimes called, the theory of comparative cost. For simplicity, he worked with two countries and two items of commodity, and measured all costs in terms of hours of labour.

Comparative advantage depends only on relative efficiencies and inefficiencies. For example a simple case where Nigeria labour has greater productivity to another using cocoa and textile. To produce a unit of cocoa in Nigeria requires a smaller number of labour days than is needed in Europe to produce it, while to produce a unit of textile takes a smaller number of labour days in Europe than in Nigeria. Thus, Nigeria will specialize in the production of cocoa and export to Europe in exchange for textile.

The principle of comparative advantage, therefore, states that whether or not one of two regions is absolutely more efficient in the production of every good than the other it will still not be profitable. If each specializes in the products in which it has a comparative advantage, trade will be mutually profitable to both regions. Real incomes of productive factors rise in both places.

If economies of mass production are overwhelmingly important, costs may decrease as output expands.

Foreign trade involves import and export.

```
                        Foreign Trade
                             |
              _____
             |                                |
          Import                           Export
```

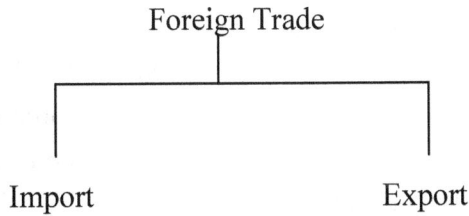

Import trade involves buying goods and services from other countries and bringing them into the country. While export trade involves the selling of goods and services to other countries.

Advantages of Foreign Trade

1. Countries with comparative advantage in the production of certain goods and services will concentrate on such production and this will lead to specialization.
2. Foreign trade will encourage mass production or will lead to increase production since there is a larger market and demand for the output.
3. It will also foster cordial relationship between countries involved in export and import of their goods and services.
4. Countries will be able to generate more foreign income which could be channeled into their economy to provide facilities for their citizens.
5. Citizens will enjoy better standard of living as assorted goods and services will be made available to them through import.
6. Increase productivity expectations will require increase labour, hence, more workers will be employed to produce enough goods and services for export.

Disadvantages of Foreign Trade

1.   It could cause unemployment if local industries are forced to wind-up or reduce work force owing to poor sales when local products cannot compete favourably with imported goods.
2.   Dependence on another country for the supply of certain goods and services could be risky in times of diplomatic break or war.
3.   Availability or dependence on foreign commodities may slow the progress towards self-sufficiency and efficiency.
4.   Foreign goods may not be as cheap as they seem, there could be dumping of sub-standard goods.

Barriers to Foreign Trade

1.   Natural barriers posed by long distance.
2.   Social and language differences.
3.   Economics arising from the need to
     -     protect home industries
     -     correct adverse balance of payments
     -     prevent dumping.
4.   Differences in currencies and exchange rates.
5.   Weights and measures differences.
6.   Political considerations, embargo, war.
7.   Government fiscal policies and administrative bureaucracies and "bottlenecks".

Balance of Trade and Balance of Payments

Nigeria's trading relationship with the rest of the world results in inward and outward flows of goods, services and

54

payments. Export from Nigeria will result in an inflow of payment, while import into Nigeria will result in an outflow of payment. The general financial results of international trade are recorded and published at regular intervals by the government statistician showing the country's balance of payment. By balance of payment, we mean the statement that takes into account the values of all goods and services, gifts, shipping services, aeroplanes, tourist expenditure, foreign aid, all capital loans, official settlements, and international reserves coming in and going out of a country. The tables record transactions referred to as current account, currency flow and financing.

Items in Current Account include:

a. **Visible Trade:** This refers to exports and imports of goods. Visible trade is also referred to as "balance of trade", such as crude oil, cocoa, machinery, vehicles, electronics.

b. **Invisible Trade:** This refers to the import and export of services, such as, postal, cable, internet, and embassies.

c. **Current Balance:** Also known as "balance on current account". Favourable balance on current account means the value of goods and services exported exceeds the value of goods and services imported.

Unfavourable balance is when total imports of goods and services exceeds total exports of goods and services.

Equilibrium is when total imports is equal to total exports, this is ever not plausible.

A favourable balance over a period of years indicates that a country is doing fine, an unfavourable balance, however, should give cause for concern since it suggests that a nation is consuming more than it is producing.

d.   **Balancing Item:** The figure is used so as to balance the account; it records the net total of errors and omissions in other items; that is, errors and omissions shows there were statistical discrepancies due to imperfect statistical information.

e.   **Drawings:** This item refers to loans especially those obtained from the International Monetary Fund (IMF).

Import Trade

Import trade involves the coordinated, numerous commercial activities which lead to the bringing in of goods from other countries into Nigeria.

Countries import goods for the following reasons:

1.   Because of climatic and other reasons no country is able to produce all the goods needed by her citizenry, nor all the raw materials or input for her industrial, scientific and technological development.

2.   There are economic advantages, since countries have comparative advantages for the production of certain goods than others. They enjoy economics of scale, mass production, low unit cost and maximization of profit.

3.   International specialization of labour occurs due to division of labour.

56

Nature has not spread her resources evenly around the world, hence, most countries find that they must depend on other countries for the purchase of items they need but cannot produce at all, or for the purchase of goods which are needed to supplement home production or that its cheaper to import from other countries than to produce.

For instance, Nigeria imports equipments, finished products for consumption, vehicles, ships, planes, trains, industrial raw materials, clothing, jewelleries, electronics and many other things and can therefore, enjoy a higher standard of living by taking advantage of the international specialization of labour. She can then concentrate on the production of item for which she has comparative advantage and specialization such as; crude oil, cocoa, groundnuts, palm oil, rubber, coal and tin.

Export Trade

Trade is a two-way affair in the modern world, and no nation can hope to sell its own goods abroad unless it is prepared to buy goods in return. A nation which wishes to import must also be prepared to export; and must keep her exports in such a quality and at such reasonable price as will enable her to achieve a balance of trade.

Export trade, therefore, involves the outflow of goods and services to other countries of the world; and is undertaken by a number of different groups including manufacturers, overseas agents, export merchants, export commission agents, export associations, chamber of commerce and industry, packaging and forwarding agents and governments.

Price Quotation

Since most of the goods traded on are many and bulky, they are usually shipped. The following Price Quotations are therefore applied.

1. Delivery or Free Docks: The charges of unloading and delivery to the docks at the port of departure are included but dock dues, wharfage and porterage are not.

2. FAS: Free along side means that the goods are delivered to the side of the ship, but that any charges for loading onto the ship are extras.

3. FOR (Free On Rail) and FOT (Free On Truck) cover all costs up to and including on rail. The buyer pays all subsequent costs, including railway and other transport charges.

4. FOB (Free On Board) a port could be named e.g. FOB Port Harcourt; includes the cost of loading the goods onto the ship. The seller will collect receipt from the shipping company and send to the buyer.

5. C & F (Cost and Freight) signifies that the freight will be paid by the seller and will secure the necessary bills of lading.

6. CIF (Cost, Insurance and Freight) the seller will pay for the freight and insurance.

7. CIFI (Cost, Insurance, Freight and Interest) in addition to the payment of freight and insurance, the seller includes interest on the value of the shipment; that is, the agent's commission is added.

8. CIF & E (Cost, Insurance, Freight and Exchange) seller's quotation which includes also the risk of exchange fluctuations and banker's charges.

9. Ex ship means that the seller will pay all expenses up to the time the goods arrive at the port of discharge, but the buyer must bear the cost of taking delivery from the ship.

10. Landed means that the seller pays all expenses on the goods up to the point of discharge, including cost involved in landing them from the ship at the named port.

11. In Bond means seller will deliver the goods into a customs bonded warehouse but that any further charges for withdrawal will be borne by the buyer.

12. Duty paid includes payment of import duties at port of delivery.

13. Franco, Rendu or Free means that all charges for delivery to the buyer's warehouse are included in the quotation.

Government Aid for Exporters

The Ministry of Commerce and Industry is concerned with promoting trade in general and export trade in particular.

Hence, the following are ways exporters are encouraged in their businesses:

1. The Ministry in collaboration with the Chamber of Commerce and Industry, supplies registered firm with current or up-to-date information about world trading situation, such as:
   a. Assessments of particular markers for particular products.
   b. Current tariff and import regulations.
   c. Current labelling and marketing requirements.

d.   Details of overseas contracts put out to tender.

e.   The commercial standing of overseas traders.

f.   Advice on exporting safeguards.

g.   Statistical data on prices, production figures, etc in various countries of the world.

h.   Safe trading countries.

i.   Forecast analyses on global market.

2. **Promotion of Overseas Trade:** Government assist exporters in this direction especially in launching or introducing a product in a foreign market.

3. **Government Activity to Free Trade:** Exported goods must be free to enter other countries and not be obstructed by tariff barriers. There are several groups of nations, each of which offers its members reciprocal trading advantages. These may be free trade areas or customs unions such as: Economic Community of West African States (ECOWAS), Niger Basin Commission (NBC), Lake Chad Basin Commission (LCBC), European Economic Community (EEC), the Commonwealth Countries, General Agreement on Tariffs and Trade (GATT) and others.

4. **Export Finance and Insurance:** Although the government cannot help directly in the finance of export, it does indirectly assist exporters. For example, through governments fiscal policies it could lower tariffs, reduce lending rates, exchange rates and even advise commercial banks to grant favourable credit facilities to exporters.

5. **Resolving Commercial Disputes:** Situations do arise when Nigerian exporters encounter problems or are

involved in disputes with their buyers, the government do intervene in such disputes and resolve such problems before they become legal.

6. The government, through the Export Promotions Council, encourages Nigerian manufacturers to export their goods. The council offers incentives such as granting soft loan facilities to exporters.

7. Through the Nigeria Export Credit Guarantee and Insurance Scheme which guarantees payments in case of default by overseas buyers as a result of non-insurable risks and non-payment resulting from wars, change of government, national disaster, political instability, embargoes and others to exporters.

8. Through Trade Fairs and Demonstrations organised by governments in conjunction with manufacturers, business organisations, chambers of commerce and industry, professional bodies such as Nigeria Society Engineers (NSE), held in both foreign and home countries to exhibit or advertise Nigerian products and potentials so that foreign investors could know what the country can offer.

9. Government also simplifies export procedures and documentations in order to encourage exporters.

10. By the establishment of export free zones, government sets out industrial areas which are meant to produce mainly for exports. Industries within the area are granted tax holiday or low excise duties.

11. Exporters are encouraged to keep their foreign exchange earnings for use in these countries.

12. Government may not charge excise duties on goods meant for export for a period. That is, granting tax holiday to local manufacturers to encourage export.

Measures Government may take to Restrict Imports

There are numerous measures government can take to restrict imports, some of which are:

1. **Imposition of custom duties** – Imposition of such taxes on imports increase their prices, thereby, discouraging importation.
2. **Granting of subsidies** – Government may give outright financial assistance to local industries to enable them produce cheaper but comparable goods to serve as substitutes to imported ones.
3. **Import licence** – Imports can be restricted by placing all goods on licence before importation can be allowed.
4. **Exchange control** – Rigid control of foreign exchange rates will make it difficult for importers to pay for goods.
5. **Devaluation of the local currency** – This reduces the purchasing power of the currency and makes imports more expensive.
6. **Enlightenment Campaign** – This is to enlighten citizens to make use of homemade goods. This campaign if vigorously pursued may discourage the patronage of imported goods.
7. **Quota** – Government may place a specific limit on the quality or type of goods to be imported or from what countries they should be imported.

8. **Embargo** – Placing an embargo or banning importation of some goods.

CHAPTER 6

BANK AND BANKING

What is a Bank?

A bank is an institution, which collects surplus funds and valuables from the general public, governmental and non-governmental establishments, safeguards them and makes them available to the true owner when required. It also loans out funds, on interest, to those who are in need of them and can provide security.

Who is a Banker?

A banker is any body of persons, whether incorporated or not, who carries on the business of banking. Its principal activities include the acceptance of money on current account, the collection of cheques on behalf of customers and payment of cheques or orders drawn on it by a customer.

Types of Bank

The following are some of the types of bank:
1.   Central bank
2.   Commercial Banks
3.   Agricultural Banks
4.   Industrial and Development Banks
5.   Co- operative and Commerce Banks
6.   Merchants Banks

7. Mortgage Banks

8. Special Banks, such as the defunct People's Bank.

Types of Bank Account

The common types of account operated in banks are:

1. Deposit/ Savings Account

2. Fixed Account

3. Current Account

Basic Functions of Banking

The basic functions of banking include:

1. The collection of surplus funds from the general public, government and non-governmental establishments.

2. The safeguarding of such funds.

3. The transfer of these funds from one person to another, without the funds leaving the bank, by means of the cheque and credit-transfer systems.

4. The lending of money, based on any surpluses available, to other customers who are in need of funds, in return for an interest and collateral security. The interest is shared between the bank (a reward for its services) and the true owner (a reward for not using his money, that is, making his money available for the bank to loan out).

Services of the Commercial Bank

Services rendered by commercial banks today cover an enormous range of activities such as:

A. **Current Account Services**

1. Transfer of money by the cheque system

2.   Transfer of money by standing orders
3.   Transfer of money by the credit-transfer systems
4.   Granting overdrafts
5.   Granting loans
6.   Providing night- safe facilities
7.   Issuing Bank drafts/cheques
8.   Receipt of deposits on current (or cheque) account

B.   **Fixed Deposit Account Services**
C.   **Savings Account Services**
D.   **Other Services:**
1.   Foreign exchange activities for importers and exporters
2.   Acting as intermediaries in dealing with stockholders
3.   Executorship and trustee services
4.   Providing safe custody for documents and other valuables
5.   Insurance services
6.   Giving income tax advice to customers
7.   Providing services for exporters
8.   Ascertaining credit rating credit worthiness of customers
9.   Providing economic information
10. Issuing bankers' credit cards
11. Discounting bills of exchange
12. Investing management services
13. Providing agency services

a. The collection and payment of cheques, bills, dividend warrants and other instruments

b. Assisting companies to raise capital, such as through sale of shares

c. Making periodic payments of subscriptions, such as insurance premiums, on behalf of customers through standing orders.

14. Issuing various types of letters of credit, credit cards, banker' cards, travellers' cheques and foreign exchange transactions.

15. Providing automatic cash dispensers, that is, making cash available when requested from personal or company account.

What is a Cheque?

A cheque is a written order drawn up and signed by the customer of the bank (drawer) on which he instructs the bank (drawee), to pay a certain sum of money to a specified person or firm (payee).

Cheques are normally made out on the printed cheque leaves provided by the bank and are for making withdrawals from current accounts only.

Specimen Cheque

(a)	(b)
Date --- (j) ---------	DAVTON BANK PLC Date --- (j) ---------
(c)	Isiohor Branch, 100 Davton Street, Isiohor, Benin. (k)
To-------------------	(c)
(e)	Pay --or Order
₦-------------------	(d)
	The sum of ---
	---₦ (e)
(i)	(f)
Balance------------	
(g) 000459912	000459912 01124317 C 0202899281
	(g) (h)

Keys:

a. The stud of the cheque that is retained after the cheque leaf has been detached, all necessary information are entered to serve as reminder of the transaction that took place pertaining to the particular cheque.

b. The cheque leaf

c. Person or firm to be paid, that is, the payee

d. The sum of money to be paid written in words

e. The sum of money to be paid written in figures

f. The owner of the account, that is, the drawer, signs his regular bank signature here

g. Cheque leaf number

h. Owner's bank account number

i. Balance amount that should be left in the account after the cheque must have been cashed.

j. Date the cheque was issued

k.   Name and address of bank, that is, the drawee

Procedure for Opening a Current Account
1.   An application is made to the bank of choice by the prospective customer.
2.   He collects the relevant forms, such as, personal data form, signature card, guarantors forms.
3.   He gets two guarantors who should, preferably, be customers of the same bank and branch to fill the guarantors forms for him.
4.   He fills the personal data forms and submits same with the guarantors forms
5.   He submits two passport size photographs (black and white or coloured, depending on the specification of the bank)
6.   He is given the paying-in-slip (teller or form) to fill indicating the amount of money to be paid in according to their denominations.
7.   He fills in the signature card by signing his signature. This is very important because this signature will be subsequently used to verify his banking transactions especially in honouring his cheques.
8.   He submits the paying-in-slip with the total amount to the receiving cashier.
9.   The receiving cashier counts the money and examines the teller entries to ascertain that they correspond and conform to the bank's requirements. If all the details are correct, the cashier will stamp, sign and handover a copy to the customer, this will serve as a receipt for the deposit made.

10.   He is then given a cheque book with his account number stamped on each leaf for his subsequent withdrawal. Some cheque books are personalized with the name and account number of the owner printed on.

Dishonoured Cheque

There are circumstances under which a cheque taken to the bank cannot be cashed or credited to the account, this cheque is said to be dishonoured.

The circumstances could be:

1.   No sufficient money in drawer's current account.
2.   Amount written in words and figures differ.
3.   When the cheque is stale, that is, the cheque judging from the date it was issued had not been cashed for six months.
4.   When there are alterations on the face of the cheque that were not endorsed by the drawer of serious mutilations.
5.   When the signature of the drawer is irregular, that is, the signature on the cheque differs from that on the banker's signature cards or that shown on the computer screen.
6.   When a post-dated cheque is presented before due date.
7.   When an account has been frozen by government or court order.
8.   When an account has been rendered dormant, as the owner had not operated it for some stipulated period, the account needs to be reactivated by the owner.
9.   When the owner of the account stops the payment of the cheque for a reason and informs the bank on time.
10.   When the payee cannot adequately identity himself.

CHAPTER 7

INSURANCE

Insurance is a contract by which one party undertakes to indemnify another against loss, damage or liability arising from an unknown or contingent event.

Insurance is another division of commerce, it is based on the principle of the pooling of risks, this means that by insuring a life or property, those who insure contribute to a common fund out of which compensation is paid to those insured who suffer loss.

The money which the insured pays is called a **premium** and it is collected from a large number of people who are insured against a particular loss. The premiums so collected make up the funds out of which those insured who actually suffer losses are compensated. All things being equal, the number of people who are insured against a particular loss should be more than those who actually suffer loss. This enables the insurance company to pay compensation and still make profits.

Principles and Doctrine of Insurance

There are three main principles of insurance, and a famous doctrine which is rather similar to a basic principle.

Insurable interest and Uberrima fides or utmost good faith apply to every contract of insurance, indemnity applies to all contracts of insurance except personal accident and life assurance. It has two corollaries, contribution and subrogation. Finally the doctrine is called the doctrine of proximate cause.

1.   Insurable Interest:

Everyone who has an insurable interest in something is entitled to insure it against any risk that may occur. To have an insurable interest we must be in danger of suffering some loss or incurring some liability should the thing concerned be destroyed or damaged in any way.

Insurance is a contract between two parties. They consist of the insurance company which is called the insurer and the person taking out the insurance who is called the insured. Under the insurance law, a person is not permitted to insure something which does not belong to him.

Insurable interest means, therefore, that only the person who will suffer financial loss if the event to be insured against occurs, will be allowed to take out insurance.

You can, therefore, insure your house, furniture, electronics, cars, jewelleries, company. because you will suffer loss should they be destroyed, damaged or stolen. You can also insure your life, your wife's, children's, and the like.

2.   Uberrima Fides or Utmost Good Faith:

When a contract is made, it is presumed that people will deal honestly with one another. The applicant for insurance must disclose to the insurance company whether asked or not, all necessary information that will assist the insurer determine whether or not to cover the risk and the premium to charge. The insurance company is also required to disclose to the proposer all facts material to the risk to be covered.

The law says *caveat emptor,* that is, let the buyer beware.

Breach of utmost good faith by the insurer or the insured renders the contract null and void at the option of the aggrieved party.

3. **Indemnity and Life Assurance:**

The principle of indemnity cannot apply in a straightforward way to life assurance, for no sum of money can equate the loss of life or any part of the body. All that these policies can do is to provide a sum of money, called the benefit payment, as compensation. Life assurance premiums are roughly related to the way of life of the insured. The insured will be adequately compensated but he is not expected to make a profit out of the insurance, that is, he will not be paid more than his normal earnings.

Corollary of Indemnity-Contribution: This provides that if a property is insured with more than one insurance company, the amount claimable from individual insurers will be limited to their individual rateable proportion of the loss.

Corollary of Indemnity-Subrogation: If the principle of indemnity says that "I must be restored to the condition I was in before I suffered the loss", it would be wrong to accept compensation and continue to have any to her rights as well. The word "Subrogate" means "to step into the place of" or "to find a substitute for."

If, for example, a car is wrecked in an accident, the insurance company will compensate the insured for the wrecked car, then the wrecked car becomes the property of the insurance company.

4.   The Doctrine of Proximate Cause:

This rule states that if we insure against a certain eventuality, we are entitled to compensation only if that eventuality is the immediate (or proximate) cause of the loss. That is, there must be a close connection between the loss actually suffered and the risk for which insurance has been taken out.

Types of Insurance:

The different types of insurance include:

1.   Marine insurance
2.   Fire insurance
3.   Accident insurance
4.   Export credit insurance
5.   Fidelity guarantee insurance
6.   Agricultural insurance
7.   Life Assurance
8.   Burglary insurance

Marine Insurance:

Marine insurance is the type of insurance covering sea transportation. It is taken out to cover ships and cargo at sea. Marine insurance is probably the oldest form of insurance and the most important given the involvement of all countries of the world in international trade.

Types of Marine Insurance Policies:

1. *Voyage Policies* – Subject matter is insured for a specified voyage, for example, Nigeria to New York.
2. *Time Policies* – Insurance is taken out on the ship for a specified period of time, usually not exceeding 12 months.
3. *Construction or Builders Risks Policies* – To cover the risk of damage to vessels during the period of construction, during trials and until delivery to the owners.
4. *Port Risk Policies* – Cover vessels whilst in port for a stated period of time.
5. *Fleet Policies* – By which several vessels belonging to one owner are insured under the same policy, for example, Nigeria National Shipping Line taking out a policy for its vessels.
6. *Composite or Combined Policies* – Which are subscribed by more than one insurance company on the one policy, stating the liabilities of each company.
7. *Mixed Policies* – Cover both voyage and for a specified period.
8. *Floating, Open or Declaration Policies* – Generally used by merchants, shipper or businessmen who regularly despatch or receive goods.

9.   *Hull Policies* – Enable ship owners to insure the ship itself against loss or damage which may be caused by fire, storm or collision with other vessels.

Management of Risks in Small Business
The Fire Danger

In view of the fact that owners of small scale enterprises go through a lot of difficulties in establishing their businesses, it is, therefore, pertinent that nothing should be left to chance in ensuring the protection of their investments.

The fire danger is a risk aspect that owners of small businesses must guide against.

The following are ways that could be employed:

1.   ***Workshops and Seminars:***   The owner of small business should periodically organize workshops and seminars for his workers internally or sponsor some of his workers to professionally organized fire prevention workshops and seminars. These trainings will equip the workers on how to prevent fire outbreak, how to use fire fighting instruments such as fire extinguishers, sand buckets, oxygen masks, water hose and hydrants, fire escape exists, etc.

2.   Provision of fire fighting gadgets such as fire extinguishers, sand buckets, oxygen masks, water hose and ensuring that water is constantly available either by tap water or provision of water in tanks, drums or other containers.

3.   ***Precautionary Measures:***   Owners of small scale enterprises should ensure that detailed precautionary

measures are taken to prevent fire outbreak. These include the following:-

a. Proper electrical wiring of the business premises.

b. Provision of electrical stabilizers to machines.

c. Electrical outlets should not be overloaded with many electrical equipment.

d. Fire-proof steel lockers or fireproof rooms should be provided for storage of valuables.

e. All electrical equipment or machines should be switched off at close of business day except for facilities that are absolutely necessary to leave such as cool-room or freezer.

f. Only trained and responsible personnel should be allowed to use electrical gadgets.

g. Faulty electrical equipment should be conspicuously marked as such, to prevent its usage by innocent workers.

h. Fire escape exists should be well marked and also location of fire fighting equipment.

i. Highly combustible chemicals or liquids such as gas and fuel should be safely keep away from fire and bold warning signs placed by them, such as "no smoking" sign.

j. The activities of neighbours or adjourning businesses need to be carefully examined as they could pose hazards to your own business.

k. Fire accident caused by lighting could also be prevented by ensuring that thunder arrester is installed on the building.

l.   Regular servicing of machineries should be carried out to prevent explosion.

m.   Personnel employed should be of proven character in order to guard against potential arsonists.

4.   *Fire Insurance Policy:* Of utmost importance for fire danger is for the owner of small business, if he can afford its, to take out a fire insurance policy. The purpose of a fire insurance policy, is to provide a sum of money in compensation for any damage that has been suffered as a result of fire that was insured against. The owner will receive compensation to indemnify him for the loss. Fire insurance began a few years after the great fire of London in 1666, when a speculative builder Nicolas Barbon started the fire office in 1680. By 1805 there were 11 fire offices in London and over 30 in the British Isleg. They have their own fire brigades and marked their own insured buildings. They sometimes will refuse to put out fire on properties not insured by them but wills standby should the fire spread to their own insured properties.

Insurance companies did not exist in Nigeria until 1921 when the royal exchange assurance company commenced business and have grown rapidly especially since Independence in 1960. The first Insurance Act was promulgated in 1961 by the Federal Government known as the Insurance Companies Act 1961. There are different types of insurance coverages of which fire insurance is one.

The main types of policy issued by the fire office are:

a. Fire insurance on domestic and business premises and their contents.

b. Consequential loss insurance: This type of policy may well be regarded as comprehensive insurance. In policy (a) above where the business premises and their contents are insured, the insured will only be indemnified to that extent. But in a fire situation, those may not only be the loss incurred, other commitments could be:

    i.   Temporary hiring of another business premise while the burnt one is being renovated.

    ii. Profits that could have been earned if the business was not interrupted.

    iii. Permanent and most valuable members of staff of the company that would be retained and their salaries.

    iv. Outstanding mortgage payments for the building (if any).

    v.   Other fixed charges such as director's fees, rent, rates licence renewal payment, interest on loans, etc which still continue even when the business premises has been destroyed.

    vi. Any price increase that will occur by taking outstanding business to another firm to execute.

All these losses will be indemnified when a consequential loss insurance policy is taken out by the owner of a small business.

The Crime Danger

Criminal incidents have been the bane of many small scale businesses. The types and manners of crimes cannot easily be enumerated as new devices crop up everyday.

Owners of small businesses may, therefore, ensure that the following precautionary measures are applied to minimize crime risk.

1. ***Recruitment of Employees:***

Managers should ensure that they meticulously adhered to strict recruitment procedure. Potential workers applications should be thoroughly screened, interview should be conducted, references checked, employment records verified to attest to the integrity of the person to be employed.

Business owner should watch out for any civil unrest or riot. Criminals could take advantage of such disturbances to loot or cause damages to business properties. In such a situation, the business premises or store should be sealed or locked up immediately. The police should also be informed immediately for assistance.

Advance payments should not be made for supply of goods except with reputable companies or suppliers. This is very important so as not to be duped by fake suppliers or fall victim of advance fee fraud (419).

2. ***Security Measures:***

   a. Only tested, reliable workers should be placed in charge of sensitive jobs, such as, bank transactions, sales personnel, cashier, store keeper, payment of salaries, custodian of accounting records and documents such as receipts books and cheque books.

   b. Sensitive documents or petty cash should be securely kept in a well-located safe or steel locker.

   c. Burglary proofs or protectors should be installed at strategic places such as windows, doors, cashier's cubicle or manager's office to prevent easy access to such places by unauthorised personnel.

   d. Security personnel could be employed such as watch day or night guard or gateman.

   e. Electronic burglar alarm could also be installed and other electronic monitoring gadgets such as camera or metal detector, assess to a telephone and police emergency number in case of armed robbery.

   f. Responsibilities should be diversified to workers as concentration of related jobs in the hands of one employee will be unwise. For instance, the same worker should not keep the cheque book, write the cheques, pay salaries and keep bank records.

g. Periodic stock-taking exercise should be conducted by manager to reconcile assets acquired, used or issued and in-stock.

h. Proper documentation of assets and liabilities of the business.

i. There should be constant supervision and monitoring of workers activities in order to discourage pilferage and suspicious characters visiting them.

j. Credit sales should be granted to only long-term trusted, reliable and established customers.

k. Cheques for payments should only be accepted after through verification to avoid dud, bad, fake or bounced cheques from dubious customers.

l. Supervisors and security personnel should be tactfully vigilant to avert shoplifting.

m. Cash payments should be carefully counted and checked for fake or counterfeit currencies.

n. Cash movement schedules should not be rigid in terms of time and route. Sporadic or flexible cash movements will make it difficult for the criminally intended mind to succeed or predict.

If the proprietor of the small business can afford it taking out an insurance policy will also be advisable. It could be theft insurance and/or fidelity guarantee insurance. A common fidelity guarantee is the commercial fidelity guarantee which is taken out on employees such as cashiers, accountants, salesmen, managers or others who have been entrusted with business funds. It should be noted, however, that the owner of the business will only be reimbursed after the employee has been charged to court, this condition is to serve as a deterrent so that the policy will not be abused.

CHAPTER **8**

BUSINESS LAW

Business law involves all the aspects of law that govern business transactions. The major emphases of business law are law of contract and sale of goods.

Contract

Contract is more than a mere agreement or premises between persons and groups, between a person and an organisation or between one organisation and an another. It is "a promise or set of promises creating a legal duty of performance."

It is also regarded as "an agreement that creates an obligation binding upon the parties thereto." Another definition states that it is "an agreement or covenant between two or more persons, in which each party binds himself to do or forbear some set act and each acquires a right to what the either promises."

Thus, in legal terms, contract is simply defined as a legally binding agreement between at least two parties, imposing rights and obligations on the parties which will be enforced by the courts.

Not all contracts or agreements are legal or enforceable in a court of law.

For a contract to be legal, there are five essential requirements as identified by Reutter and Hamilton (1976).

They are:-
1. Mutual assent (i.e. there must be an offer and also acceptance).
2. Consideration
3. Legally competent parties
4. Subject matter not prohibited by law, and
5. Agreement in form required by law.

In all cases, the promise or promises (offer and acceptance) which are the bases of the contract must be made voluntarily.

As contract is, therefore, said to be void, voidable or unenforceable if it lacks any of the essential ingredients.

1. **Mutual Assent:**

Offer: Before parties enter into a contractual relationship they usually engage in informal negotiations, which may or may not result in a contract depending on whether the parties were able to reach a mutual agreement or not.

To have an agreement, two or more persons must arrive at a mutual understanding with one another; a party makes a proposition and another acceptance of that proposition. The party making the offer, *the offeror*, makes a proposal to the other party to whom the offer is made, *the offeree*, who is to consider stated conditions.

An offer to contract is composed of two parts:

a.   An expression by the offeror of what he promises shall be done or happen or shall not be done or happen, and

b.   An expression of what the offeror demands in return.

The offeror may communicate his proposition to the offeree by acts, orally, written or by any combination of these. Since a contract is based on an obligation voluntarily assumed, the offeror must make his proposition with the intent to contract, thus making *intent* an essential element of an offer.

As a general rule, the courts have held that an advertisement of goods for sale of a stated price is not an offer to sell the goods at that price, that it is merely an invitation to negotiate for the sale of the goods. However, if an advertisement contains a positive promise and statement of what the advertiser demands in returns, the courts will generally hold that it is an offer.

Termination of Offer

Duration of offer when an offeror makes an offer, he confers on the referee the power to create a contract by the acceptance of the offer; but for practical and legal purposes, such power cannot exist for an indefinite period of time. The power to convert an offer into a contract may be terminated in the following ways:

1.   By provisions in the offer

2.   By lapse of time

86

3.   By revocation

4.   By rejection of the offer by offeree

5.   By death or insanity of the offeror or offeree

6.   By destruction of the subject matter of the proposed contract, or

7.   By the performance of the proposed contract becoming illegal.

Acceptance: Acceptance must be unconditional as the basis of a contract is the mutual consent of the parties concerned. The offeror made a proposition and the offeree indicates either expressly or by implication, his willingness to be bound on the terms stated in the offer. The offeree, has no legal right to insist that the proposition made to him be altered.

The common law rule is that the offeree's acceptance must correspond in all respect with the offer.

The offer can be accepted only by the person to whom it is made or organisation, and acceptance must be communicated by words or positive conduct.

Acceptance must be within the time stipulated or within a reasonable time.

2.   **Consideration:** This refers to the price which each side pays and the advantages or benefits each side enjoys for the promise or performance of a contract. That is, both the offeror and the offeree give or promise to give something of value to one another, this valuable consideration could be money, goods, services or giving up of a legal right.

A consideration is *quid pro quo* i.e. something for something.

3.   **Legally Competent Parties:** This is also referred to as legal capacity of the parties. The term "capacity" denotes the ability to perform legally valid acts, that is, the ability to incur legal liability or to acquire legal rights.

Since some persons, due to natural incapacities, are considered incapable of protecting their interests in our free competitive economy. Parties have capacity to contract are essential to the validity of a contract and there must be at least two persons – the promisor and the promisee – as parties to a contract. An individual cannot contract with himself, nor can he as an individual contract with himself as an official.

Persons with natural incapacities to perform legally valid acts are under legal incapacities such as, drunken persons, aliens, corporations, minors, convicts, sick and mentally unstable people, do not have full legal capacities. Similarly, at common law, a married woman could not contract as her legal existence ceased when she married, the husband becomes the sole representative of the family.

4.   **Subject Matter Not Prohibited by Law:** A bargain is illegal if either its formation or its performance is detrimental to the general public interest. The individual's right to bargain is recognised and protected, but public welfare supercedes individual rights, and whenever the bargain of individuals is criminal, tortuous, or contrary to accepted standards of morality, it will be declared to be illegal and will not be enforced

by court action. Illegal bargains are generally declared to be void.

There are an infinite number of situations which give rise to illegal bargains, however, they are generally classified into the following categories:

a.   Bargains in violation of positive law
b.   Bargains made void by statute, and
c.   Bargains contrary to public policy – requiring immoral or unethical act.

a.   ***Bargains in violation of positive law:*** The commission of a crime or a tort is a violation of positive law. If the formation or the performance of a bargain requires a violation of positive law, it is illegal. For example, four sole-proprietors may decide to form a partnership, this is legal. But if the partnership is formed to create a monopoly so that they can charge higher prices, then the bargain is a violation of positive law and, therefore, illegal.

b.   ***Bargains made void by statute:*** The statutes affecting the legality of bargains may be divided into three classes:
       i.   Criminal statutes
       ii.   Statutes expressly declaring contracts void, and
       iii.   Regulatory statutes

c.   ***Bargains contrary to public policy:*** Bargain's opposed to public policy vary so greatly that it is impossible to list them. Public policy changes from time to time depending on social political and economic developments, conduct which may be acceptable in one period may not be acceptable in another time and vice versa. A bargain, the performance of which would require the doing of an immoral or unethical act, is illegal. There is no simple standard or rule that could be used in the court of law, each case is treated according to available facts and the presiding judge has broad discretionary powers in determining whether or not a bargain is against public policy and illegal.

The public policy of a state or nation is reflected in its constitution, laws, and judicial decision.

5. **Agreement in form required by law:** The statutes of fraud require "a memorandum" or "a note or memorandum" or "a contract in writing". It may be in any form, such as, a formal contract, letters, telegrams, receipts or any other writing accurately stating the material provisions of the contract.

The memorandum or note may consist of several documents, which must be attached physically or by the content or references in the documents themselves, that they all refer to the same transaction. If a contract in writing is required, it must include all the material provisions of the agreement, and must be made with the intent to bind the party signing it.

90

1.   The names of the parties or designate to them so that they can be identified from the content of the writing;
2.   Must describe the subject matter of the contract with reasonable certainly;
3.   Must state the price to be paid (with some exceptions) and must state credit terms, if credit is extended;
4.   All other terms that are material.

Tort: Legal injury or wrong committed upon the person or properly or another independent of contract.

Negligence: Lack of care.

Slander: Defamation by spoken words.

Libel: Defamation by printed or written communication.

Defamation: Scandalous words written or spoken concerning another, tending to the injury of his reputation, for which an action on the case for damages would lie.

Classification of Contracts

To aid in the analysis of contractual problems, contracts have been classified according to their various characteristics.

1.   **Formal and Informal or Simple:**   Contracts under seal, negotiable instruments and recognisances are classified as formal contracts. All other contracts, whether oral or written, are classed as informal or simple contracts.
2.   **Unilateral and Bilateral:** As the terms indicate, a unilateral contract is one in which only one of the

parties makes a promise, whereas in a bilateral contract, both of the contracting parties make promises. For instance, a promise to pay a reward for the return of lost property is a promise for an act. And a promise to repay money loaned is an act for a premise. The lender performs the act of giving the loan and the borrower promises to repay the money.

A promise to sell and deliver goods given in exchange for a promise to pay the agreed purchase price at some future date is a bilateral contract or a promise for a promise.

3. **Valid, Unenforceable, Voidable, Void:** A valid contract is one which fulfils all the   legal requirements for a contract. A court will lend its aid to the enforcement of a valid contract.

An unenforceable contract is one which satisfies the basic requirements for a valid contract, but which the courts cannot enforce because of some statutory requirements or rule of law. For example, a contract which is oral, but which, if it is to be enforceable, is required by statute to be in writing, is unenforceable.

A voidable contract is one which binds one of the parties to the contract but gives to the other party the right, at his election, to withdraw from the contract. For example, a person who has been induced by fraudulent representation to make a promise is given the right to elect not to be bound by his promise.

A void contract is a nullity due to lack of some essential elements of a contract, that is, it has no legal force or effect.

92

4.   **Executed and Executory:** A contract becomes executed when all the parties to the contract have fulfilled all their legal obligations created by the contract. Until all such legal obligations have been fulfilled, the contract is executory. If one party partially fulfils his obligations, the contract is regarded as partially executed.

If one party has fully carried out his own part of the obligations, then the contract is executed to him and executory to the other party yet to fulfil his own part of the bargain.

5.   **Express and Implied:** An express contract is one in which the promise or promises are stated or declared in direct terms. That is, all the ramifications, expectations and obligations of the contract will be clearly stated either orally or written.

An implied contract is one in which the promise or promises are not stated in direct words but are gathered by necessary implications or deductions from the circumstances, the general language or the conduct of the parties. For example, a person orders for certain goods to be supplied to him and does not discuss payment, it is implied that he will pay the standard price for the goods.

Termination of Contracts

A contract may be terminated in the following ways:

1.   **Execution:** A contract may terminate when all the parties involved have fully completed their obligations as stated in the contract.

2. **Mutual decision of the parties:** Owing to circumstances beyond their control, parties to a contract may mutually agree to terminate the contract even though the contract has only been partially fulfilled.

3. **Breach of contract:** Breach of contract occurs when one party or both parties to a contract did not fulfil the anticipated terms of the contract. With an improvise in the contract that the agreement is voidable if certain obligations are not fulfilled, the aggrieved party can sue seeking for compensation for damages, or enforcement of certain obligations or outright termination of the contract.

4. **Government laws and policies:** There are situations when government laws and policies can render a contract void. Laws and policies are not static, what is applicable in one period will not be in another period, hence, contracts entered into in one period could be made void in another period due to the enactment of new laws and policies or amendment to existing ones. These include, fiscal policies, import/export regulations, income distribution and socio-political interplay.

5. Other reasons such as death, serious illness or medical reasons could also terminate a contract.

CHAPTER 9

INVENTORY

In a manufacturing organization, one of the functions of the production manager is to ensure that the inputs for production are readily available in both quantity and quality. The objective of the production manager is to maximize the value created and the production system is the framework within which the creation of value can take place.

Figure 3   Production Process

Inputs Human	Creation of value	Output which
Non-human	through manipulation,	added value
No	transformation,	over the value
	conversion of inputs	of the inputs
	Modification	Evaluation
	feed back	satisfactory
		Yes

Raw materials are important inputs into the production system and an effective and efficient production Manager will ensure that the raw materials are deadly available for production at the right time, right quantity and right quality. Inventory or stock keeping is a management function of ensuring that the required raw materials are available for production.

Types of Inventory are:

1.   Production - Raw materials
2.   Maintenance, Repairs and Operating supplies (MRO)

(Work-in-Progress)
3.   (In-Process) – these are semi-finished products found at various stages in the production operation.
4.   Finished goods – these are completed products ready for the market.

Problems of Inventory

The following are some of the problems of Inventory:

(a)   Wastage during production
(b)   Rampant pilfering
(c)   Poor storage
(d)   Inefficient record keeping
(e)   Poor security
(f)   Obsolescence
(g)   Poor quality purchase/supply
(h)   Supply time lag (disappointments)
(i)   Government policies – especially for imported raw materials – exchange rate and effect on payment for goods – not encouraging local Raw Material Sourcing

Functions of Inventory Stores include the following:

1.   To receive and maintain custody of raw materials, spares, tools, work-in-progress and finished goods.
2.   To issue the materials when required
3.   To account for stock
4.   To determine adequate storage facilities
5.   To assist in stock taking
6.   To advise management

7.   to liaise with sub-stores and other departments.

Inventory Management Techniques

-    Economic Order quantity
-    `Re-order level
-    Minimum stock level
-    Maximum stock level

Methods of pricing materials issued from Store are:

1.   First in First Out (FIFO)
2.   Last in first Out (LIFO)
3.   Simple average price (cost of total batches/number of batches
4.   Weighted average price
5.   Standard price
6.   Market price
7.   Inflated price
8.   Highest in First Out (HIFO)
9.   Next in First Out (NIFO)
10.   Base Stock Method

Figure 4   Inventory Process

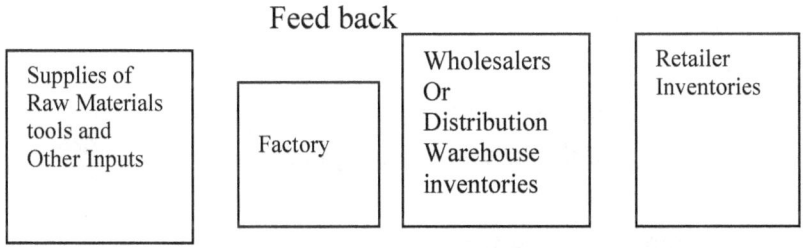

Feed back

Supplies of Raw Materials tools and Other Inputs	Factory	Wholesalers Or Distribution Warehouse inventories	Retailer Inventories

Inventory Process

Inventories make possible a rational production system without them we could not achieve smooth production flow,

97

obtain reasonable utilization of machines and reasonable service to customers.

At each stage of both manufacturing and distribution, inventories serve the vital function of decoupling the various operations in the sequence beginning with raw materials, extending through all of the manufacturing operations and into finished goods storage, and continuing to warehouses and retail stores. Between each pair of activities in this sequence, inventories make the required operations independent enough of each other that low-cost operations can be carried out: thus, when raw materials are ordered, a supply is ordered that is large enough to justify the out-of-pocket cost of putting through the order and transporting it to the factory.

Similarly, in distributing finished products to warehouses and other stock points, freight and handling costs per unit go down if we can transport in large quantities.

Procedure for Stock Acquisition

The purchasing officer having decided that there is need to purchase stock, will prepare the requisition order. Then the following procedures will be followed:

1. Get it approved
2. Mailed or sent to factory (supplier)
3. Received at the factory (by supplier)
4. Filling the order
5. Loading, trucking (transporting)
6. Received at the warehouse
7. Cross-checking and unloading into the warehouse

Although we have one set of costs that is fixed by the purchase or production order size and another set of costs that increases with the level of inventory, normal warehousing procedures are to prepare a procurement order to the factory (supplier) when the warehouse inventory falls to a critical level called the order point.

Kinds of Inventories

Pipeline Inventories: The warehouse must, at a minimum, carry enough stock on hand to meet demand during the transit time.

Lot Size or "Cycle" Inventories: Since the goods have to be transported from the factory to the warehouse, the logical question is "how many to transport at one time". The lot size, therefore, varies from situation to situation; while overhead costs are being considered such as the costs preparing requisition and other clerical costs.

Buffer Inventories: The period of making requisition to delivery of goods is usually not constant, so a buffer stock is normally required to protect against unpredictable variations in demand and supply time.

Decoupling Inventories: These make the required operations independent enough of each other so that low-cost operations can be carried out. For example, the existence of inventories at the retail level makes it possible to carry on that function relatively independently, replenishment stocks are ordered only periodically. The existence of separate inventories provides the needed independence between stages.

Seasonal Inventories: Many products have a fairly predictable but seasonal pattern through the year. Where this is true, management has the choice of changing production rates over the year to absorb the fluctuations in demand.

The Purchasing Officer must adhere to the Following Guidelines:

1. Supply sources must be dependable to win business.
2. Buyers may favour loyal suppliers, by patronising them always.
3. Buyers must spread their risk, by buying from more than one supplier.
4. Buy at Economics Order Quantities (EOQ).

Figure 5 Relation of total cost (including storage) per unit to quantity ordered.

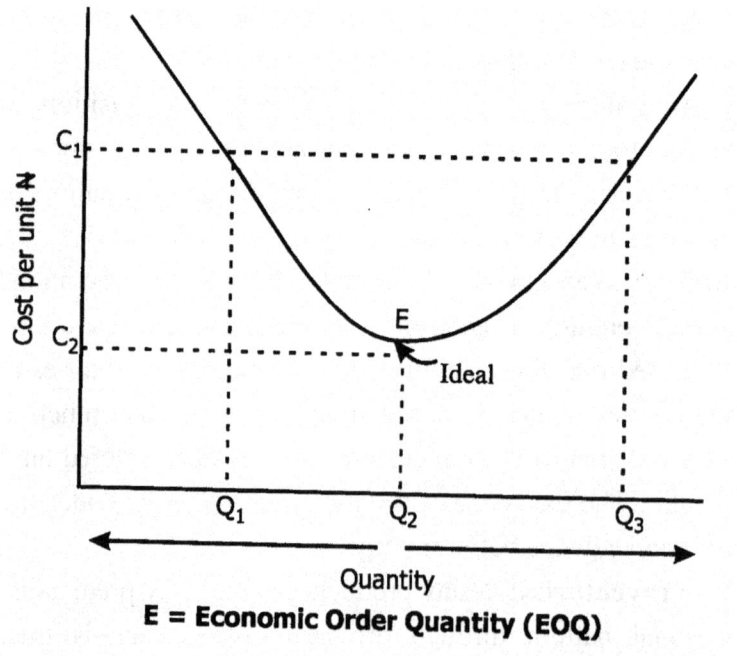

E = Economic Order Quantity (EOQ)

Some Factors that Cause the Curve to Decline as the Quantity Purchased Increases are as follows:

1. Price discounts are sometimes given as quantity purchased increases.
2. Transportation costs are usually lower as the quantity transported increases.
3. Purchasing costs may be relatively fixed per order, not per unit ordered. As quantity increases, therefore, the per unit ordering costs decreases. An average purchase order may cost ₦1,000 to ₦2,000 regardless of the number of items ordered.

The Following Factors Cause the Curve to Rise and Suggest the Purchase of Appropriate Quantities:

1. Interest, insurance and taxes will be higher on larger quantities held in inventory.
2. Space costs will be higher, especially if additional warehouse space must be rented or built.
3. The risk of deterioration and obsolescence of inventory are increased as the quantity held in inventory is increased.
4. There are fixed rates no matter the quantity purchased. Cost will be high if lower quantities are purchased or if excessive quantities are purchased.

The ideal point is the equilibrium point, where cost and quantity meet at the lowest point on the cost curve.

CHAPTER **10**

PRODUCTION

Man, no matter his country, state of origin and cultural background has always needed things from birth to death. All man's life, he will be needing one thing or the other, such as, drink when thirsty; food when hungry, clothing and more. People have, therefore, learnt how to satisfy their needs in different ways. Some are hunters, fishermen, cattle rearers, doctors, teachers, farmers; while others have developed and discovered complex methods of doing things so that output rises and they become wealthy.

The basic needs of man are:

1. Food
2. Water/drink
3. Clothing
4. Shelter
5. Land
6. Medical care

With the advent of western civilization, man's needs have become more sophisticated and varied, some want to be pacesetters in fashion, others want sleek cars, tape-recorders, coloured television, video players/recorders, lasers, cellular phones, radios, washing machines, swimming pools, tennis courts, travelling by air, personal computers, assorted meals

102

and drinks, houses and a lot more than the ordinary needs of everyday.

All the wants of man can be **classified** as **"goods"** and **"services"**. Goods are material items or **tangible goods** that can be handled such as cars, clothes, food, furniture and house.

Services are intangible such as the services of teachers, barbers, entertainers, postal and telephone services, lawyers, bankers, doctors, drivers, cooks, administrators, entertainers and tailors.

The provision of goods and services is called production. Production has to take place in order to satisfy human wants.

There are two methods of production:

1. Direct – sole producer.
2. Indirect – producing by specialisation.

Direct production indicates that a man can satisfy all his wants entirely unaided by other people. This is a very inefficient form of production as there is a limit to what a man can produced all alone.

Indirect production involves everyone, and each one specialising in what he knows best, that is, there is division of labour.

Advantages of specialization are:

1. People choose the work they like or are competent in.
2. They save time by using the same equipment all day.
3. The specialist becomes more skilled because of repetition.
4. He inverts new tools.
5. These tools can be mechanized.

6.   Ensures greater output.

Types of Production
The three main types are:
1.   Primary production
2.   Secondary production and
3.   Tertiary production.

The table below shows the classification of producers or specialists who work in the three types of production.

Types of Production

(Extractive) Primary	(Constructive/ manufacturing) Secondary	Tertiary	
Natural wealth	Conversion of natural wealth of goods	Services	
Coal miners	Engineers	Commercial	Personal
Gold miners	Builders	Wholesalers	Doctors
Tin miners	Carpenter	Retailers	Dentists
Lead miners	Plastic engineers	Bankers	Teacher
Oil drillers '	Aeronautical engineers	Importers	Nurse
Farmers	Textile/fashion	Insurance	Policemen
Fishermen	Tailors	Agent	Entertainer
Herdsmen		Ship crew	Editor
Wine tappers		Captain	Author
			Barber

The first recognised attention to production economics was paid by the great Scottish economist – Adam Smith at the time the factory system was emerging. In 1776 he wrote **The Wealth of the Nations** in which he observed three basic

104

economic advantages resulting from the **division of labour**. These are:

1.   The development of a skill or a dexterity when a single task was performed repetitively.

2.   A saving of the time normally lost in changing from one activity to the next; and

3.   The invention of machines or tools that seemed normally to follow when men specialized their efforts on tasks of restricted scope.

In 1832, Charles Babbage, an Englishman augmented Smith's observation, also Frederick Taylor with "Scientific Management."

Babbage's thoughts were summarized in the book *On The Economy of Machinery and Manufactures* (1832) concerning the economic advantages resulting from the division of labour.

The current rate of development of production management concept, theory and technique began shortly after the World War II.

This talk about the new look in production management is fine for the big company, but what about the small-scale ones?

The owner's primary **function** is to make decisions that determine the future course of action for the enterprise over the short and the long terms. These decisions may be directed in every conceivable physical and organizational area, they may deal with financial planning, marketing and personnel, as well as with the operating or production phase.

Figure 6   Production Function Model

Design of production systems

↓

Planning for production

↓

Implementation of production plans

↓

Control of operations

Quality   Quantity   Productivity

Resources	
Human	Non-human

Production management is, therefore, a set of general principles for production economics, facility design, job design, schedule design, quality control, inventory control, work measurement, cost and budgetary control.

What is Production?

Production is the process by which goods and services are created. Production management, then, deals with decision

106

making related to production processes, so that the resulting goods and services are produced according to the specifications, in the amounts and by the schedule demanded, and at minimum cost.

a. The first concern of the production manager is to provide inputs to the production system such as plant facilities, materials and labour. That is, to acquire machinery and equipment, raw materials and production workers.

b. Once the inputs have been assembled, the creation of value can take place. This is the stage where the production manager's attention is mostly needed such as:

i.   scheduling jobs on machines.

ii. assigning labour to jobs

iii. controlling the quality of production.

iv. improving methods of work.

v.   handling materials efficiently so as to avoid waste.

c. The final stage of production is the completion of output when the finished products or services are made available for consumption.

Production Process

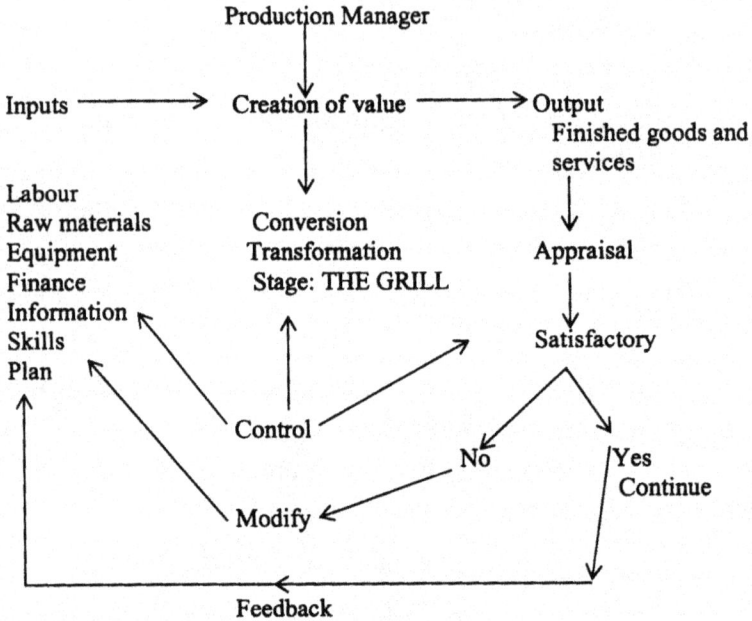

Production Manager

Inputs ⟶ Creation of value ⟶ Output
Finished goods and
services

Labour
Raw materials   Conversion
Equipment   Transformation   Appraisal
Finance   Stage: THE GRILL
Information
Skills   Satisfactory
Plan

Control

No   Yes
Continue

Modify

Feedback

It should be noted that for all these various activities to be effectively coordinated and carried out, there must be in place effective information and communication system.

Production management function is generally or essentially about producing goods and services on time, in the right quantity, right quality and by the most efficient means, that is, minimum cost.

The scope of production activities varies from one business to the other depending on the nature and complexity of operations. For instance, the activities involved in the bakery may not be as intricate and delicate as those of processing table

108

water or in computer business, or those of a fashion house with specialised and custom made demands.

Control must be a continuous assessment or appraisal of activities. Comparing actual performance with set goals and standards to ascertain compliance or otherwise. If there are variances or deviations, then necessary modifications will be made promptly to avoid wastage and loss of goodwill.

Production Planning

This involves making decisions about the work that ought to be done in the planning period whether on the short or long-term.

Such decisions have to be communicated to the affected workers that will be involved in the production process – such as, the store-keeper, purchasing officer, supervisor, machine operator and other workers.

There must be detailed arrangements for the job scheduled, inputs required must be established, such as, raw materials in both quantity and quality; labour and equipment for the efficient production of the output.

Plant Location

Location of the plant decision is very important, if the balance of cost factors is to be taken into consideration. Factors to be considered include:

- Availability of infrastructure, such as, good roads, rails, communication system, light and water, which are crucial for effective production.
- Nearness to raw materials.
- Nearness to labour

- Nearness to market
- Nearness to financial services
- Availability of other servicing outfits for maintenance of machines, spare parts, schools, health services, fire station, police station and transportation.

Problem areas of production management are:-
1. Selection and design of products.
2. Selection of equipment and processes
3. Production design of items processed
4. Job design
5. Location of the system
6. Facility layout.
7. Inventory and production control
8. Maintenance and reliability of the system
9. Quality control
10. Labour control
11. Cost control

Job Design

The effective management of both human and non-human resources of an organization will go a long way in determining the realization of its objectives. But the importance of the human resource cannot be over-emphasized. The design of the employee's job and the general nature of job assignments will relate to how effectively this human resource is utilized.

Job design is important to managers because the way jobs are structured, designed and coordinated has a direct and significant impact on the performance of the organization. Factors to be considered include the number of employees

110

required to accomplish a particular task; the type of task; the required skills; abilities, training, authority, responsibilities and the level of supervision required, are all related to job design.

Job design, therefore, could be defined as related to "the content, functions and relationships of jobs that are directed toward the accomplishment of organizational purposes and the satisfaction of the personal needs of the individual job holder."

As this definition reveals, job design is concerned with a number of aspects of an individual's job. Among these are the job content, the requirements of the job, the required interpersonal relationships, and the performance outcomes, as shown in the figure below.

Figure 8: **A Framework For Job Design**

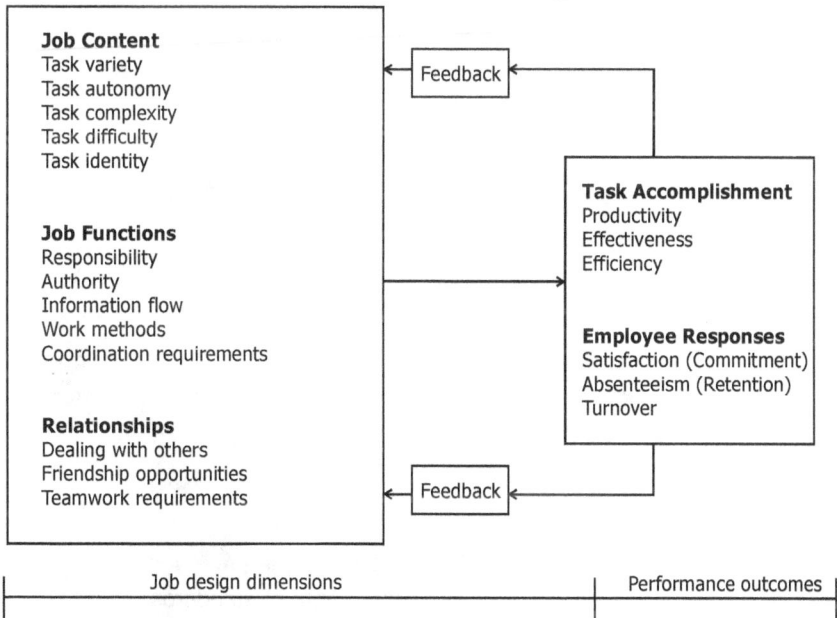

Job Content
Task variety
Task autonomy
Task complexity
Task difficulty
Task identity

Job Functions
Responsibility
Authority
Information flow
Work methods
Coordination requirements

Relationships
Dealing with others
Friendship opportunities
Teamwork requirements

Feedback

Task Accomplishment
Productivity
Effectiveness
Efficiency

Employee Responses
Satisfaction (Commitment)
Absenteeism (Retention)
Turnover

Feedback

Job design dimensions   Performance outcomes

Adapted: Szilagy & Wallace (1980:148)

111

The job content includes those aspects that define the general nature of the task or work.

The job functions are the requirements and methods involved in each job.

Relationships concern the interpersonal components of the individual's job.

Performance outcomes concern the level of job performance.

Feedback from the outcomes of the job generally originates from two sources:

(1)   Direct feedback from working on the task, and

(2)   Feedback from other individuals, including peers, superiors or subordinates.

Figure 9:   Performance Review Cycle

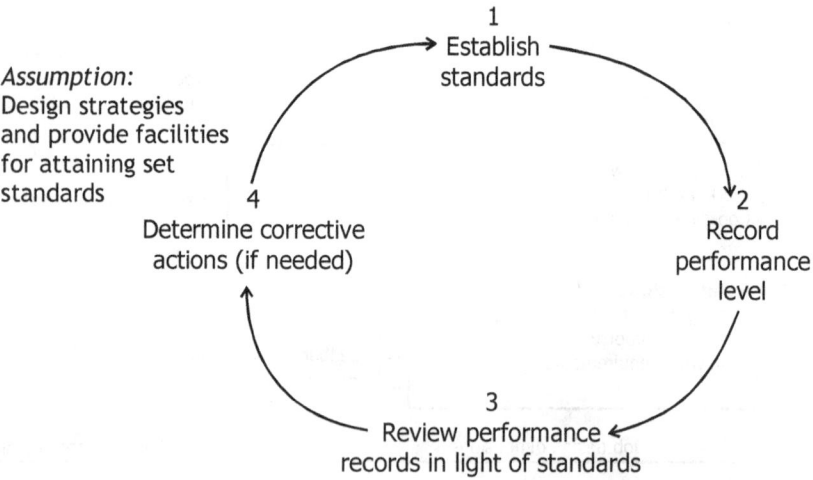

Performance appraisal or evaluation serves at least the following purposes.

1. Promotion, separation and transfer decisions.
2. Feedback for the employee regarding how the organisation views his performance.
3. Evaluation of relative contributions made by individuals and entire departments in achieving higher-level organizational goals.
4. Reward decisions, including merit increases, promotion and other rewards.
5. Criteria for evaluating the effectiveness of selection and placement decisions.
6. Ascertaining and diagnosing training and development needs for individual employees and entire divisions within the organization.
7. Criteria for evaluating the success of training and development decisions.
8. Information upon which work scheduling plans, budgeting, and human resources planning can be based.

The performance appraisal is, however, based on the assumption that the organization designed strategies and provided facilities for attaining the set standards.

Figure 10: Purposes of Job Analysis

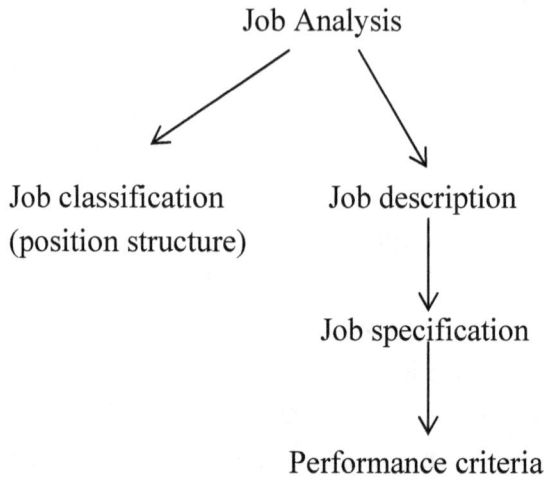

Job Analysis

Job classification
(position structure)

Job description

Job specification

Performance criteria

Job analysis is a procedure for gathering the judgement of people who are knowledgeable about the organization, the position within it, and the specific content of a job. It consists of defining the job and discovering what the job calls for in employee behaviours.

Job description – specifies responsibilities and reporting relationships.

Job specification – indicates employees characteristics and qualifications that are required in order to perform the job adequately: such as skills, knowledge, capacities, attitudes and education.

CHAPTER 11

MARKETING

Marketing is concerned with designing an efficient and fair system which will direct an economy's flow of goods and services from producers to consumers and accomplish the objectives of the society.

Marketing is the performance of business activities which direct the flow of goods and services from producer to consumer or user in order to satisfy customers and accomplish the company's objectives.

Marketing is also defined as those activities which are involved in the identification of consumer needs and the mobilization and organization of both human and material resources for the satisfaction of these needs at a profit to the company.

Another definition states that marketing is the management function which organizes and directs all business activities, involved in assessing and converting the customer purchasing power into effective demand for a specific product or service and moving the product or services to the final consumer so as to achieve the profit target of the company.

In summary, marketing can, therefore, be regarded as the management process, which identifies, anticipates and supplies customer requirements efficiently and profitably. It involves human activities directed at satisfying needs and want through exchange processes and finally, it is concerned with research and development, product policy, production planning, quality control, stock holding, credit, price policy, after–sales services, sales organization and manning the selling function. It is also involved with choice of distribution channels, dealer policies, advertising, branding, packaging and personal contact between any employee and a customer. Marketing should begin with the consumer not with the production process. Marketing and not production should determine what products are to be made including decision about product development, design, and packaging, what prices are to be charged; where and how the products are to be advertised and sold.

There are a number of possible ways to satisfy the needs of target customers. A product can have many different characteristics such as colour, appearance, package of various sizes, colours, materials, of shapes; brand names, sales and after – sales services. Various advertising media may be used; prices, cash/ trade discounts; company's salesmen may be employed, different distributive channels may be used; and credit policies may be adjusted.

With so many variables to contend with, it is necessary to reduce them to four basic ones viz:

Product
Place
Promotion and
Price

Which are referred to as the "four P's".

Fig 11: Emphasizes their interrelationship and their focus on the customer

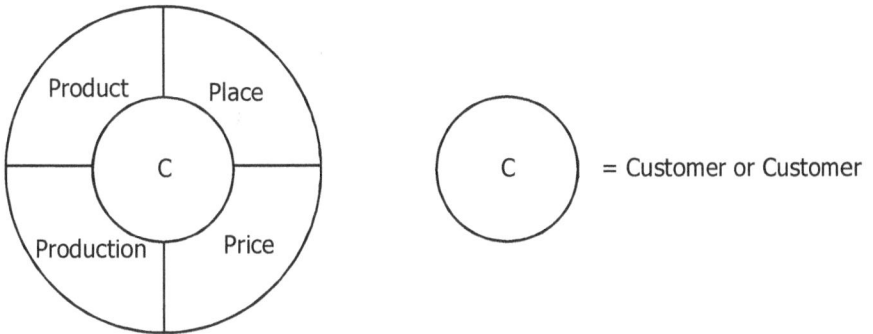

All four P's are essential to the marketing mix, in fact, they are interdependent.

Who is a Customer or Consumer?

1. A customer is a person who brings us his wants. Our job is to fill them profitably to him and to ourselves.
2. He expects value in what he buys from us. If we do not give him value, he will go elsewhere to find it.
3. A customer's good opinion of a business organization is the most valuable asset in the world. It cannot be bought or stolen, it has to be earned, and hence, whatever we can do to build that good opinion will eventually be to our advantage.
4. A customer is the boss behind our boss. By serving him well, we serve ourselves as well.

The overwhelming importance of the customer and a customer orientation is suggested by the following question from a booklet distributed to production employees by a large industrial organization in the United States of America.

It pays to be customer minded. He is never too far away to affect our jobs, no matter how remote from him our work may seem. One small slip or flaw in any department can lessen the value of our product or service in the Customer's eyes.

The customer is variously referred to as the consumer, client, user or purchaser.

Figure 12: Marketing Manager's Framework.

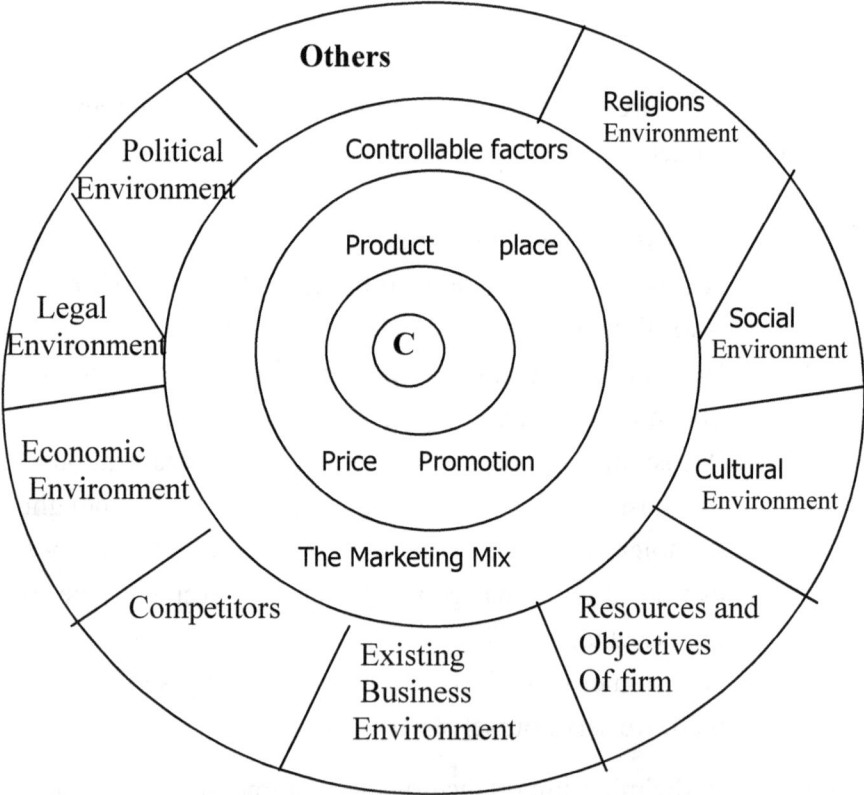

Uncontrollable Factors

118

Organization Chart of the Marketing Department

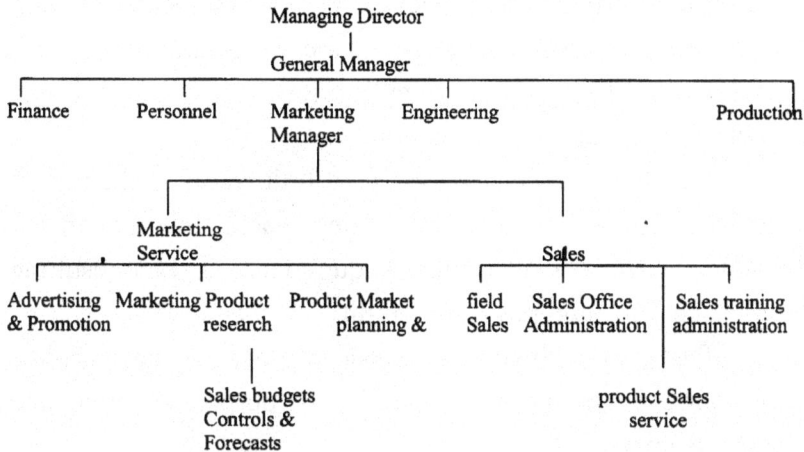

Managing Director
|
General Manager

| Finance | Personnel | Marketing Manager | Engineering | Production |

Marketing Service

| Advertising & Promotion | Marketing Product research | Product Market planning & |

Sales budgets
Controls &
Forecasts

Sales

| field Sales | Sales Office Administration | Sales training administration |

product Sales
service

Place/Physical Distribution

A product may be the best in the world, but it will be of little use to the customer if it is not where he wants it, when he wants it.

Place provides time, place and possession utility. The development of a satisfactory product provides form utility, but this is of little time and place utility to permit possession utility.

Physical distribution is the handling and moving of physical goods within individual firms and through channel systems. Transporting and storage should be considered within the channel, hence, when developing a marketing strategy, the marketing manager must determine precisely how these functions are to be carried out since this will affect the other three Ps especially pricing.

Distribution Trades:

The distributive trades form the last link in the chain of intermediary activities involving the transfer of goods and

119

service from producer to consumer.

Since production cannot be considered complete until the product is in the hands of the consumer, the work performed by the distributive trades must be viewed as a vital aspect of the process of production.

Goods in the warehouse are of little value to the person who requires them, except when they reach him through the wholesaler and retailer and have acquired added value resulting from place, time and possession utility.

Distribution involves the sale of goods to intermediate consumers, that is, those who buy for the purpose of resale and final consumers.

Functions of Distributive Trade

1. They hold stocks of goods until required.
2. They provide variety in choice by promoting or displaying a wide selection of merchandise
3. They provide vital market information relating to trends, which can be valuable to producers and consumers.
4. They add utility to goods by making them available for the consumer at time and places to suit him.
5. Packaging/ wrapping bread, oil soap tied in smaller sizes/ quantities.

Channels of Distribution

A channel of distribution has been described as the sequence of institutions listed in order of their participation as buyers, sellers or holders of products in providing the facility to move those products from producer to consumer.

Thus, when goods move from the manufacturer (m) to the wholesaler (w) from him to the retailer (r) and from him to the consumer (c) the course taken by title to the goods (m → w → r → c) constitutes a channel of distributions. Channels may be classified according to the number of stages in ownership thus:

1.   A one – stage channel is constituted where the manufacture supplies the consumer directly.

2.   2 stage channel manufacturer supplies retailer directly and he in turn supplies the consumer.

3.   3 stage channel manufacturer supplies the wholesaler, who supplies the retailer, who in turn sells to the consumer

4.   4 stage channel manufacturer supplies an agent (primary wholesaler), who supplier wholesaler, (secondary wholesaler) who then supplies Retailer who supplies the consumer.

Figure 6

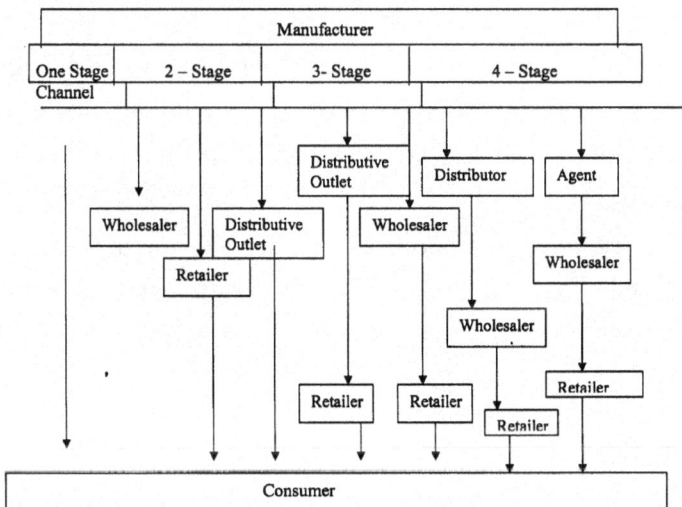

Transportation

Transportation in business is the actual physical distribution of goods. It involves the movement of goods from the manufacturer to the consumer. It also moves passengers geographically, such as traders and their goods going to market for the exchange of goods and services. Transportation is part of tertiary production, satisfying wants by making goods available and by giving services to those who need them such as individuals, families on businesses, holidays, amusement, to travel for their day-to-day affairs.

It also enables a fuller use to be made of the division of labour, because transport increases the size of a market, the manufacturer through transportation is able to move his surplus goods from one place to the other and thereby creating more markets and making goods available to many customers.

It also encourages a higher degree of specialization as manufacturers can concentrate on the production of goods for which they have comparative advantage and exchange such goods by transportation in the market.

Transportation makes possible an increase in the scale of production, since there is market for the goods, there will be continuous production so that the wealth of the whole nation increases.

By enabling consumers in one area enjoy goods produced in other geographical locations, transportation enhances the standard of living of the citizenry.

Forms of Transportation

The principle forms of transportation in Nigeria are by Land – that is, roads and railways, Air, Water and pipelines.

Ownership of the transport system could be governments, that is, Federal, State or Local government; private individuals and firms; and public or commercial carriers.

Publicly owned operating units make up the vast majority of the road transport, local and international water transportation.

The government-owned transport systems serve both private and commercial purposes, for example, the Presidential Jet is privately used by the Presidency while the Nigeria Airways planes are used commercially to convey passengers and goods within the country and internationally. There are also bus transport systems owned by Federal, State and Local Governments. The train system is presently completely owned and operated by the Federal government for conveying passengers and goods within the country; and also owns some ocean liners for international routes.

The privately owned transport systems are those solely owned and operated by individuals and companies for the purpose of conveying their own staff and products from one place to the other. Examples of these are Uniliver Lorries and Newspaper vehicles used to convey their staff and products all over the country.

The public or commercial carriers could be general or contract carriers. This system of transportation exists when individuals and firms purposely purchase cars, buses, lorries, boats, planes for commercial uses.

The general carriers are in designated terminals for the general public to use in conveying themselves and goods to various destinations.

Some of these public carries can be contracted by producers to provide them with transport services; hence, they serve specific clients and are not disposed to the general public.

In determining the form of transportation to use in conveying staff and goods, certain factors have to be taken into consideration such as:

1.   *The commodity itself:* The weight, size and cost, is it fragile, perishable, delicate, flameable, and the quantity to be conveyed.

2.   *The staff:* The calibre, cost, distance and number of staff to be conveyed will influence the mode of transportation.

3.   *Destination:* The destination of the goods will also determine mode of transportation. If the distance to be covered is far or near, if it could be reached by road, rail, water or air and in most cases by a combination of two or more methods in international ventures or the riverine areas of the country.

4.   *Delivery:* Failure to deliver goods when needed could cause a lot of embarrassment, disaffection or even litigation. For example, one can imagine the embarrassment an intending couple could face if their wedding cake or gown were not delivered at the right time. Similarly, a company that is expecting its raw materials needed for production to be delivered at a particular time, fails to receive them; the company

124

might be compelled to stop production thereby leading to loss of personnel, overhead and even good will.

5. *Cost:* In business, a major aim is to minimize cost so as to be reasonably profitable. This cost consideration is an important factor in deciding on which form of transportation to utilize. Such reasoning are: could it be more economical to buy our own delivery van since we make supplies regularly? Our vehicle will be maintained, our staff will accompany the goods and thus guarantee safe delivery, our driver as a staff, will be careful and so on. Or will it be cheaper and more convenient to contract the delivery function to commercial carriers? All alternative methods will be analyzed and costed and the most suitable will then be utilized. Whatever decision that is made will be constantly reviewed in line with social, political, economic changes and type of commodities.

6. *The Customer:* The Customer is often referred to as the boss behind the boss. Sometimes his choice of transportation could be the overriding determinant of the mode of transportation.

Road Transport

Road transportation is one on land. It is the most highly used means of transportation.

The modes of road transport are by car, lorries, buses, trailers, trucks, tankers, motorcycles, bicycles, and carts and even by walking.

Advantages of Road Transport

1. Intermediate terminal handling is eliminated by door-to-door delivery. The operator's terminals is under his personal direction and control.

2. Road Transport is extremely flexible, operators can convey people and goods to the farthest hinterland, cities, both national and international. They can make numerous stops and do not require special terminals unlike trains, ships and aeroplanes.

3. There are specialized vehicles of great varieties to suit variety of goods. They include specialized vehicles for bulk haulage, containers, timber; tankers for fuel, diesel, gas, bitumen, chemicals, water, tipper trucks for conveying sand, granites and other types of vehicles and loads.

4. Low capital requirements are a feature of the industry, which allows a new transporter to start with a single vehicle.

5. It is very easy to get road transportation, as they are very many.

6. It helps to extend the producer's market as his goods can be conveyed from his factory to other markets and places both nationally and internationally especially within a continent.

7. It encourages mass production, as producers are able to transport their products to numerous markets, take advantage of economics of scale and specialize.

8. Transport make improved living standards possible, as consumers no longer depend on what is available locally.

9.	It adds place utility to the goods by making them available where and when they are needed.

10.	It enhances the general efficiency with which commercial enterprises are operated and transportation ensures supplies of raw materials and other necessary inputs, conveying staff to work on time enables staff and management to be mobile and carry out necessary duties and others which cumulatively enhances productivity and profitability.

The Storing Function/Warehousing

Storing is the marketing function of holding physical goods between the time of production and the time of sale or final use. It provides time utility.

Storing is necessary because production does not always match sales or consumption. Some products are produced regularly throughout the year in anticipation of demand and to ensure that these goods are available for the consumer all year round, they must be stored.

Storage, therefore, permits price stabilization throughout the consuming period. In Nigeria, mostly non-perishable products are stored as our technology for processing and preserving perishable goods such as agricultural commodities is not yet advanced and widespread.

Warehousing encourages wholesalers and distributors to purchase goods in large quantities in order to get quantity discount from producers.

Warehousing also enables manufacturers and middlemen to keep stocks at convenient locations ready to meet customers' needs.

Goods are also sometimes stored as a hedge against future price rises, strikes, shipping interruptions, and other disruptions: and when demands are seasonal as with raincoats and umbrellas. It may be related to a particular festival, like the demand for greeting cards, decorations, gifts and toys at Christmas period. Inspite of the advantage of storing, these benefits cannot always be achieved, especially in developing countries where adequate storage facilities are not available or even non-existent.

Types of Warehouses

1. **Private or branch Warehouses:** These are those owned by individual companies for their own use. Most manufacturers, wholesalers and retailers have some kind of storage facilities. The management of a manufacturer's finished goods warehouse is often the responsibility of the Sales Manager.

    Private warehouses are used when a large quantity of goods must be stored regularly. Owning a private warehouse, however, can be expensive both for construction and maintenance.

2. **Public or Commercial Warehouse:** These are warehouses owned by government or private individuals or companies, built purposely for hiring by manufacturers who do not need permanent warehouses.

    The customers pay only for the spaces they use. Public warehouses are useful to manufactures who must maintain stocks in many locations, including foreign countries.

Some public warehouses provide all the services that could be obtained in the company's own branch warehouse or from most wholesalers, for example, they will receive the goods in large quantities from the manufacturers, unload and store them, they will inspect the goods, package and even invoice customers, and later reship them in any size lots ordered by the company or its customers. The public warehouse is also responsible for the loss of the products in the warehouse.

3. **General Merchandise Warehouse:** Store almost kind of manufactured goods. A special form of warehouse is the bonded warehouse used for storing imported goods or other goods, on which taxes or duties must be paid before the goods are release.

4. **Commodity Warehouse and Cold–Storage:** Warehouse are designed specifically for storing perishable or easily spoiled products such as fish, fruits, butter, beef and vegetables.
    Grains such as beans, rice, corn (maize) are stored in huge elevators.

Importance of Warehousing to Business

1. Some Warehouses are centrally located thereby reducing the cost of transportation in general

2. It enables wholesalers to break bulk for retailers.

3. Warehousing assists in retrieving of the goods that are either contaminated or had become obsolete.

4. Goods awaiting payment of custom duty are usually kept in bonded warehouses.

5.   Warehousing encourages mass production and the producer is assured of a place to store the goods, this will also encourage continuous production.

6.   It makes it possible to store seasonal goods until they are required.

7.   Warehousing constitutes an essential aspect of production to cater for time lag between, production and consumption or demand.

8.   It helps to stabilize price during scarcity and surplus.

9.   It provides protection and security for goods till needed

Promotion

Promotion is communication between seller and buyer. It is one of the four major variables with which the marketing manager works; and it is his job to combine all of the possible promotion ingredients into a blend which tells target customers that the right product is available at the right place and at the right price.

The basic, broad objectives of promotion are to inform, persuade or remind target customers about the company's marketing mix and the company itself.

The company must define its promotion objectives if its promotion is to be effective, because the right blend depends on what is to be accomplished.

For instance, a firm with a distinctly new product may not have to do anything but inform consumers about its offering and show them how it is better than existing products.

For products already in the market, the firm must not only inform customers that a product is available but also persuade and remind them to buy its products.

As population continues shifting geographically, as changes occur in the age, educational, occupational social and cultural characteristics of the population; and as more and more competitive products come into the market, reaching and convincing target customers become more difficult and expensive.

Basic Promotion Methods

The marketing manager may have to work with several promotion objectives at the same time, and might also be implementing several strategies at the same time and, therefore, has to plan to get across many different messages to different target customers. Normally, he uses a blend of three basic promotional methods:

1.   Personal selling
2.   Mass selling and
3.   Sales promotion.

1.   **Personal Selling:** This involves direct face-to-face relationship between sellers and potential customers the Salesman is often a very important part of this promotion method because he can adapt the company's marketing mix to the needs and circumstances of each target market and to each potential customer.

Face-to-face selling provides an immediate feedback which helps the salesman to adapt effectively.

Since the need and preferences of individuals vary greatly, the flexibility offered by personal selling requires a skilled salesman to adjust to all these target market differences.

2. **Mass Selling:** Mass selling is designed to communicate with large numbers of potential customers at the same time. It is not as flexible as personal selling where the salesman uses immediate feedback to adjust his presentation but it is much less expensive especially if the target market is large and dispersed. Advertising is the main form of mass selling.

What is Advertising?

Advertising is any paid form of non-personal presentation of ideas, goods, or services by an identified sponsor. It involves the use of such media as the following;

Magazines and Newspapers:

Poster, signs bill boards, calendars, branded biros, key-holders, motion pictures, direct mail, store signs, radio, television, directories and references, circulars, free samples, and window displays. Publicity is another form of mass selling, public relations efforts can contribute to mass selling at relatively low cost.

Trade magazines or newspapers may write or carry articles featuring the products of a company and publicity may generate far more inquires than the company's advertising.

The company's managing director or chief executive may attend a public occasion such as a football match, project launching, social ceremonies or be special guest on television, he will be introduced or constantly referred to in connection with his company and products and thereby being given "free" publicity.

3.   **Sales Promotion**

Sales promotion is another tool of promotion. It refers to specific activities which can make both personal and mass selling more effective, by coordinating and supplementing both efforts.

Sales promotion personnel may design and arrange for distribution of gifts, point-to-purchase materials and premiums, store signs, posters, catalogs, directories, circulars and reference. They assist in the development of displays, sales demonstration, trade fairs, exhibitions, jackpot or sweepstake (raffle draws) contests and coupons designed to get customers to try the product.

The company can also sponsor programmes such as football matches, sporting competitions, television programmes, scholarships, health and cultural activities.

It is difficult to generalize about sales promotion efforts because they are custom designed for the specific needs of each company and the target market.

Promotion, therefore, requires effective communication in order to get the attention of the target audience or it is wasted effort. It should attain its goals by making consumers aware of the existence of new products, services and ideas and the continued existence of old products. It should inform and educate the consumers on how to make use of the product and services, where to obtain and adopt them.

The ultimate aim of any company is for consumers to adopt its products, services or idea. Consumers need vary and their buying behaviours are regarded as a problem solving process in which they go through several steps on the way to adopting (or rejecting) an idea, product or service. Consumers learning take place during this process and if the experience with a certain product is satisfying, then habits may be formed and may lead to brand insistence or preference stage, where promotion would only remind the customer about the product and where it can be obtained. For instance, there are varieties of milk, detergents, toilet soaps and toothpastes in the market, yet consumers will insist on the purchase of particular brands inspite of their prices.

There are six stages in this adoption process: awareness, interest, evaluation, trial, decision and confirmation. These state in the adoption process dovetail very neatly with an action oriented framework – called AIDA.

The AIDA framework consists of four fundamental and interrelated promotion tasks which have been recognized for many years:

1.	To get attention	3.	To arouse desire and
2.	To hold interest	4.	To obtain action

The relationship of the stages of the adoption process to the AIDA promotion tasks can readily be seen below:

Adoption process	AIDA tasks
Awareness	A – Attention
Interest	I – Interest
Evaluation)	
Trial)	D – Desire
Decision)	

134

Confirmation)   A – Action

Obtaining attention is obviously necessary if the potential customer is to become aware of the company's offering. Holding interest gives the communication a chance to really build the prospects of interest. Arousing desire favourably affects the evaluation process and obtaining action and includes encouraging trial and subsequent adoption.

Continuing promotion is needed to confirm the adoption and assure continuing action.

Factors Affecting Selection of a Promotion Blend

Most business organizations develop a promotion blend of some kind because the various methods complement each other.

Each promotion blend is designed to accomplish the firm's overall objectives. But the particular blend selected depends on a number of factors including:

1.   The promotion budget
2.   Stage of product in its life cycle
3.   Target of the promotion
4.   Nature of the market situation and
5.   Nature of the product

1.   The Promotion Budget

Size of promotion budget affects promotion efficiency. Advertising on network radio and television may reach more people more economically than local media, but the minimum charge on network media may force smaller firms or those with small promotion budgets to use the less economical alternative.

2.   **Stage of Product in its Life Cycle**

The stage of product in its life cycle will also determine the type of promotion blend adopted. Product life cycle or stage are introduction, market growth, market maturity and sales decline. During the stage of introducing a new product, the basic objective is to inform.

At the second stage, promotional emphasis must shift from stimulating primary demand to stimulating selective demand by persuading customers to buy and stay with the company's product.

In the market maturity stage, promotion becomes increasingly persuasive rather than informative. Firms which have achieved a strong customer franchise are able to use reminder-type of advertising.

While at the last stage, the total amount spent on promotion may decrease as firms attempt to cut costs and remain profitable.

3.   **Target of the Promotion**

Promotion can be directed to four different groups: final consumers, industrial customers, retailers and wholesalers; each requiring different promotion blend.

The vast number of potential final consumers necessitate consumer goods manufacturers, wholesalers and retailers to use mass selling in their promotion blends.

136

Industrial customers are much less numerous than final consumers, hence, personal selling could be used as they may have specific questions or might need adjustments to the total product.

The promotion blend for retailers and wholesalers are very similar except that wholesalers are less numerous and more conscious of demand and cost. Sales promotion activities, mass selling are valuable, but the bulk of the promotion effort is by personal salesmen.

Then certain question have to be asked; such as, is the product for the men, women, youths, children, wealthy, masses, urban or rural people? Timing is also important, is it rainy season, dry season? If on television, is it day time or night? If newspaper, is it front page, back or where? Is magazine or journal the appropriate channel?

4.   Nature of the Market Situation

Firms in monopolistic competition may use mass selling because they have differentiated their product: but as the market tends toward pure competition, it is difficult to generalize what will happen as competitors in some markets aggressively seek to "out promote" each other, using mass or personal selling or both. The only way for a competitor to stay in such a market is to match rival promotional efforts; some companies may even resort to price-cutting and reduce funds for promotion. But once a firm is in pure competition where all producers are equal and oligopoly control of the market by a few producers, no one producer being dominant, then, there is less reason to promote the product.

5.   **Nature of the Product**

The customer's view of the product affects the promotion blend.

An extremely technical industrial product will require personal selling by a technically trained salesman who can explain and obtain feedback on how industries can use it. But for consumer goods, mass selling can be employed, as the goods are not so complicated.

Degree of brand familiarity: if the product has already won a strong brand preference, perhaps after years of satisfactory service in the market, there may be no need for aggressive personal selling. Reminder type advertising is usually adequate.

Aggressive advertising will, however, be required for new products or products whose brand names are not well established.

Product categories and promotion blend.
I.   Convenience Goods:
    a.   *Staples:* Food and drugs need mass selling.
    b.   *Impulse goods:* Need well-placed displays. They usually require highly persuasive personal selling by the retailer.
    c.   *Emergency goods:* Regarded as necessities for special circumstances, thus, little consumer

promotion is needed, except to remind buyers of its availability when an emergency occurs.

II.   Shopping Goods:

    a.   *Homogeneous goods:* These are compared primarily on price thus; the emphasis is not on low-price but to sell the products and not the particular brand

    b.   *Heterogeneous goods:* These are compared by consumers in a broader light than price alone.

The quality and other differences are highlighted.

    Promotion blend could include mass selling, retail sales personnel, and personal contact.

III.   Specialty Goods:

    Mass selling is used, such as billboards, television and newspaper advertisements, simply to remind customers of where they could be purchased. The favoured status of these products makes it relatively easy to promote them, as consumers want that particular product or nothing else.

IV.   Unsought Goods:

    Aggressive informative and persuasive promotion blend must be employed. Mass selling, personal contact, demonstrations, displays and gifts and even offer promotional pricing deals.

Product

The chief executive has an unending duty to ensure the development of products, and product lines to satisfy the ever changing desires of customers. This involves developing the right product, which then can be put in the right place, and sold with the right promotion and price.

Developing the right product is not an easy task, not only are customers' needs and preferences changing, but competition also makes products easily obsolete.

A product then, is not just a composition of raw materials but must possess the capacity to provide the satisfaction, use, or perhaps the profit desired by the customer. The total product is more than just a physical product with its related functional and aesthetic features. It includes accessories, installation, instruction on use, the package, conditions of sale, after sales service and perhaps fulfills some psychological needs. The total product may not even include a physical product at all but services, such as those provided by teachers, lawyers, doctors, and barbers.

How the consumers perceive the product has an important bearing on how much they are willing to buy. Economists have been concerned with how consumers perceive products because this affects how they select among alternatives; within their available resources.

The consumer is likely to buy more of a product at a lower price than at a higher price. This interaction of price and quantity is called "the law of diminishing demand". This law holds that if the price of a commodity is raised, a smaller quantity will be demanded; conversely, if the price of a commodity is lowered, a greater quantity will be demanded.

Figure 15: Inelastic demand

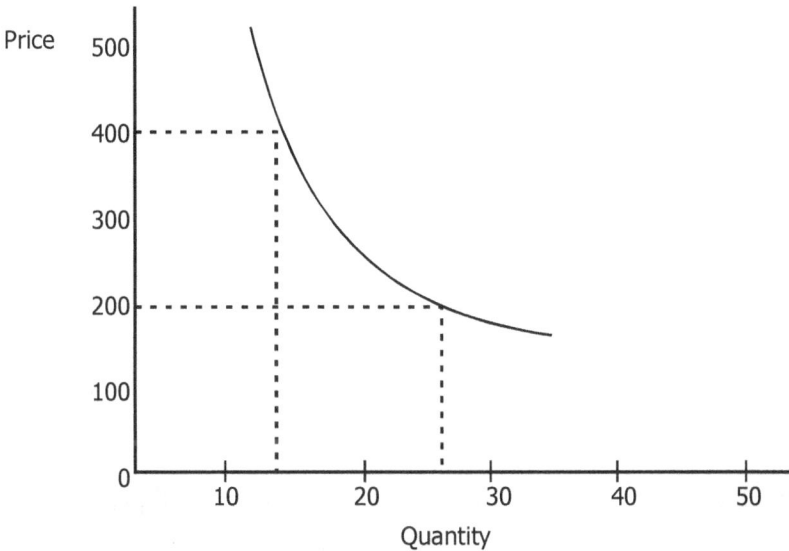

This is inelastic demand, as total revenue would decrease continually if the prices were reduced. This means that although, the quantity demanded would increase, the quantity demanded would not "stretch" enough to the increased total revenue.

In contrast, as shown below, the quantity demanded would stretch enough to increase total revenue as prices were dropped. This demand curve is an example of elastic demand.

Figure 16: Elastic Demand

Price

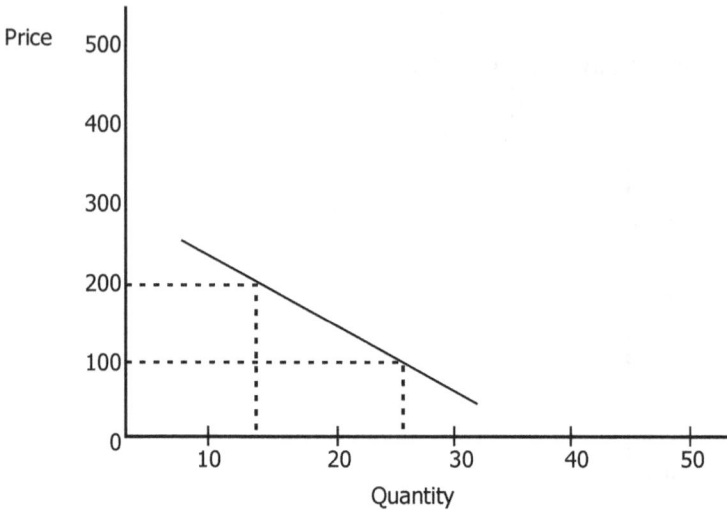

Quantity

Thus, elasticity can be defined in terms of changes in total revenue. If total revenue would increase if prices were lowered, then demand is said to be elastic.

However, in an elastic demand situation, total revenue will decrease if the price is raised while in an inelastic demand situation, total revenue would increase if the price is raised. If total revenue remains the same when prices change, then we have a special case known as **unitary elasticity of demand.**

It is important to note that it is wrong to refer to a whole demand curve as elastic or inelastic, rather, elasticity for a particular curve refers to the change in total revenue between two points on a curve and not along the entire curve.

Figure 17: Changes in Total Revenue as Prices Are Increased

A. When demand is elastic, a price increase decreases total revenue

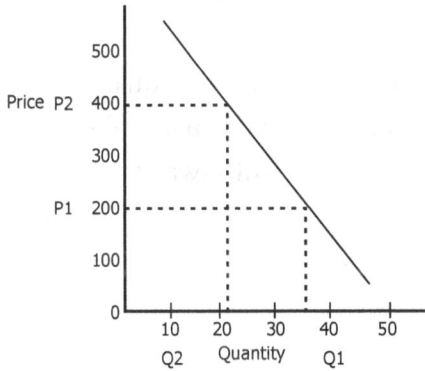

B. When demand is inelastic, a price increase increases total revenue

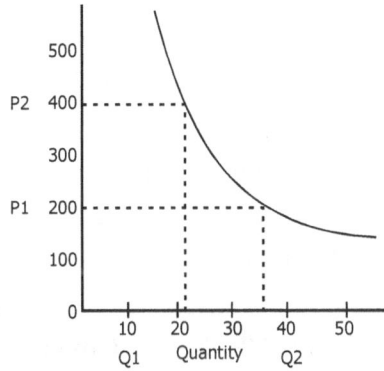

Time A

Total revenue =

$P_1 \times Q_1 = ₦200 \times 35$ units

$= ₦7,000$

Time B

Total revenue =

$P_2 \times Q_2 = ₦400 \times 10$ units

$= ₦4,000$

Time A

Total revenue =

$P_1 \times Q_1 = ₦200 \times 35$ units

$= ₦7,000$

Time B

Total revenue =

$P_2 \times Q_2 = ₦400 \times 28$ units

$= ₦11,200$

The demand curves have been discussed because the degree of elasticity is a characteristic of a particular time period. It summarizes how potential customers feel about the total product and whether there are substitutes for the product.

To have a fuller understanding of the product market situation we must continue this economic analysis by examining the suppliers willingness to supply.

While a demand curve shows the quantity of goods customers would be willing to buy at various prices, a supply curve shows the quantity of goods that will be supplied at various prices by suppliers.

Suppliers will be willing to offer greater quantities at higher prices and if a very low price is being offered, its reasonable to expect that producers will switch to other products or reduce supply. Perishable goods, however, must be sold quickly.

Figure 18: Supply Curve

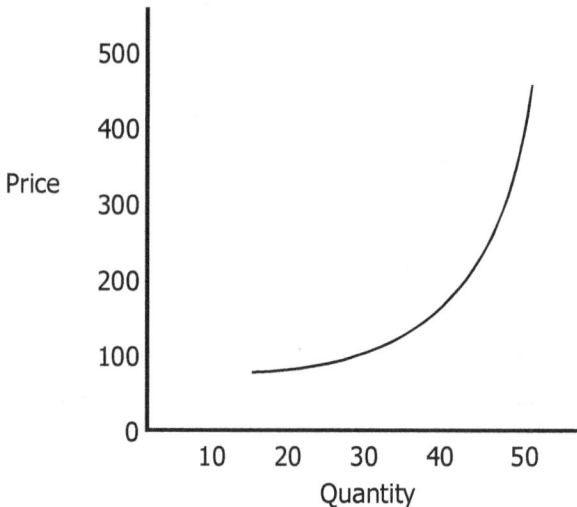

Demand and Supply Interaction

The interaction of demand and supply forces determines the size of the market and the market price, at which point of intersection, the market is said to be in equilibrium.

The intersection of demand and supply is illustrate below

Figure 19: Equilibrium Point

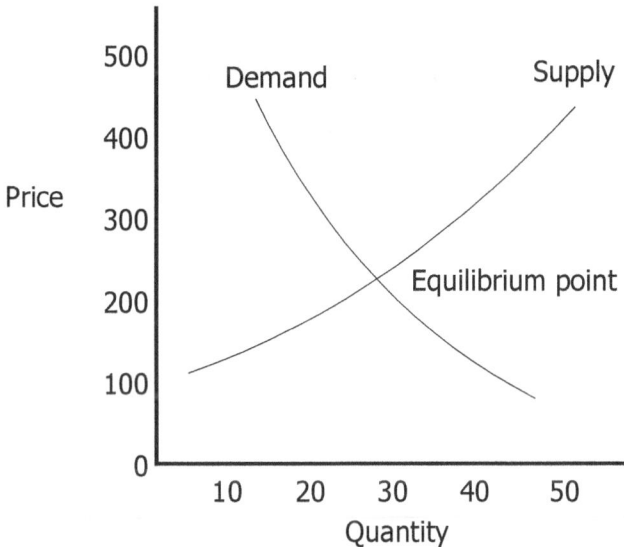

The market price is at the equilibrium point, where the quantity and the price that sellers are willing to offer are equal to the quantity and price that buyers are willing to accept.

Product Life Cycle

Some products, like consumers have life cycles. The life of a product can be divided into five major stages: Product introduction, market growth, market maturity, sales decline and product senility.

During these stages, the product's marketing mix must change because

(a)   The customers attitude may change

(b)   New target markets may be appealed to, and

(c)   Consumption pattern might change because of the nature of competition. Moreover, the profit situation changes, sales and profit do not necessarily move together. Profit may decline while sales rise or vice versa. But generally, their relationship can be seen in the figure below.

Figure 20: Stages of Product Life Cycle

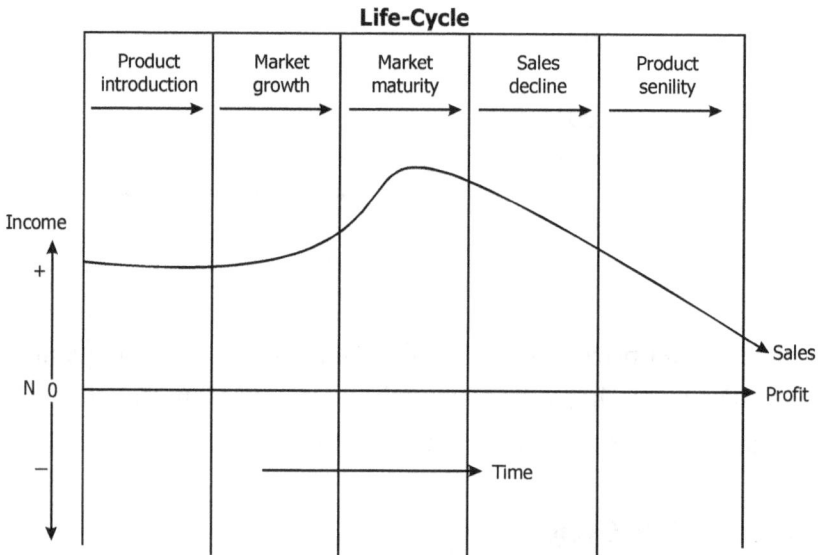

Stage I: Product Introduction

When a new product gets to the market, a company needs promotion to pioneer the acceptance of the product. The marketing manager's job is to combine all possible promotion ingredients into a blend which tells target customers that the right product is available at the right place, at the right price, stating advantages, and uses.

146

The product may not be an immediate success, this introductory stage in usually characterized by losses, with much money spent for promotion, product and place developments. These investments are made with the expectations of future profit.

Stage II: Market Growth

During this stage, the sales of the product are rising fairly rapidly as more and more customers enter the market and also the beginning of profit.

This market growth may be short-term or long-term depending on customers acceptance of the product and available variety introduced by competitors coming into the market.

Stage III: Market Maturity

By the market maturity stage many competitors have entered the market, competition gets rougher with declining profit. Promotion becomes very keen with emphasis on advantages of particular brand.

Promotion costs become very high and some competitors begin to lower prices to attract customers. Sales will begin to decline as the product reaches a period of maturity. Some producers may seek new target market or ways of prolonging the product by research development.

The market maturity period may continue for many years until a new product idea comes to completely change the market.

Stage IV: Sales Decline

In this stage of the product life cycle, new products enter the market. Both sales and profit decline at a very rapid rate, prices of dying products become more competitive, although, brand, products with customer franchise may still make profit till the end.

Stage V: Product Senility

As new products are introduced to the market, the old ones begin to fizzle out of the market.

The old products may retain some sales perhaps by older people or more conservative buyers who might slowly switch to the new products.

The total life span of a product may vary from a few days to several years, the probable length of the cycle will depend largely on strategic planning of the marketing mix.

Price

Price is one of the four major variables that the marketing manager controls. His price decisions affect both the organization's sales and profits. The needs and preferences of each target market will suggest or even establish certain price policies.

Price has many dimensions. It gives the alert marketing manager an opportunity to tailor his marketing mix to his target markets.

When a price is quoted, it is related to some assortment of goods and/or service. Any transaction in our modern economy can be thought of as an exchange of money the money being the price for something. This something can be a physical product in various stages of completion; with or without after sales services, quality guarantees, installation and instruction services.

If the product is made available to channel members, that is, stages of the distribution channel instead of final users or consumers, the price may be set so that each of the channel members has a chance to cover his costs and make a profit when he sells it at a higher price.

The nature and extent of this product will determine the amount of money to be exchanged. Final consumers may pay the suggested list price or may be able to obtain significant discounts or allowances because something is not provided. Note, however, that the price been referred to is an equilibrium price related to the forces of demand and supply; and basic list prices are the prices that final consumers or industrial users normally are asked to pay for goods.

In determining the list price many factors come into play. Usually, purchase orders specify place, time, method of delivery, freight costs, insurance, handling and other incidental charges; these are calculated and the costs will be additional to cost of production and profit margin.

Some customers get discounts off list price, these discounts are reductions from the list price that are granted by a seller to a buyer, who may either forego some marketing functions or provide the functions for himself.

Types of Discount

Types of discounts that could be granted to buyers are:

1.   **Quantity Discounts:**

Sellers offer quantity discounts to induce customers to purchase goods in larger quantities. This enables the seller to get more of the buyer's business or shift some of the storing functions to the buyer or reduce transport and selling costs, or all of these.

There are two kinds of quantity discounts: cumulative and non-cumulative.

(a)   Cumulative discounts apply to purchasers who buy over a long period of time, usually a year. This is intended to encourage the buyer to continue for a long period to buy from the same company.

(b)   Non-cumulative discounts are quantity discounts for a single purchase and do not tie the buyer to the seller beyond one purchase.

Quantity discounts may be given in the following ways:

(i)   Monetary value for instance 10% discount on goods purchase valued more than ₦50,000 or 15% on above ₦100,000 purchase.

(ii)   Number of units purchased, for example:

Units	Discounts
20	5%
50	10%
above 50	12%

(iii)   Size of purchase, that is, a purchaser who buys a trailer or luxurious bus gets a 30% discount, while one who buys a car gets 15%.

150

Quantity discounts are usually given in cash but sometimes are given as free or bonus goods, for example a customer may receive one more shirt for every twelve shirts purchased.

2. **Seasonal Discounts:**

These induce buyers to stock goods earlier than immediate demand would necessitate. This discount tends to shift the storing function farther in the distributive channel.

Seasonal discounts are also granted during low sales period for certain goods that are off season, such as post Christmas, Id El–Fitri, Easter, school reopening, holidays.

The special price reductions are also given when perishable goods or products are in season, such as oranges, corn, tomatoes, pineapples, onions and groundnuts.

3. **Cash Discounts:**

Nigeria, for now, is a predominantly cash economy especially at the retail transactions level. Cash discount may not be given for small purchases but are given for purchases of major items whose payments will, spread over a long period. Payments for such credit purchases are usually due monthly. To encourage buyers to pay promptly, the following terms of payment are frequently used:

(a)   *1/10 net 30:* means that 1% discount off the face value of the invoice is permitted if the invoice is paid within 10 days. Otherwise, the full face value is due within 30days. After the expiration of that 30 days and payment is not made, interest will be charged;

(b)   *E.O.M.* means "end of month" and given free credit to the end of the month; for example 2/5 net 30 E.O.M. for goods purchased and invoiced September 2 can have 2%cash discount for a month to October 5;

(c)   *R.O.G. or A.O.G.* means receipt of goods or arrival of goods. Under these terms, the discount period begins the day the purchaser receives the goods; that is 2/10 net 30 R.O.G. The discount method is exceptionally fair for purchasers in very far locations from the seller to make allowance for transportation delays.

Cash discounts are given to encourage buyers to pay their bills promptly and thereby enable the company to obtain its money more quickly, and to reduce credit risk and smart buyers take advantage of them.

Pricing objectives are somewhat different from the other three objectives in that they flow more directly from company level objectives which may constrain pricing by the marketing manager. But haphazard or unimaginative handling of this variable is not likely to lead to maximum profits or any other specific objective except by chance.

Price Determination

A firm can establish its price in a number of ways, but determining a price is not as easy as it seems, as the sales volume of a firm is highly dependent on fixing the most appropriate price. Some of these pricing techniques are as follows:-

1. **Cost Oriented**

   Cost-oriented pricing is quite commonly used because most accounting systems accumulate the costs of doing a particular job; and profit and loss account shows very clearly that all costs must be covered. Costs, therefore, provide a floor below which prices cannot go generally.

2. **Mark-Up Pricing**

   A chain of mark-up determines the price to the consumer. The producer's selling price to the wholesaler becomes the wholesaler's cost, the wholesaler's marked-up selling price to the retailer becomes the retailer's cost and the retailer's mark-up cost becomes the retail-selling price. Each mark-up is expected to cover the expenses of selling and administration and to leave a profit, see example below using mark-up as percentage of selling price.

Selling price = N150 = 100%	Selling Price = N200 = 100%	Selling Price = N250 = 100%
Mark-up = N30 = 20%	Mark-up = N50 = 25%	Mark-up = N50 = 20%
Cost = N120 = 80%	Cost = N150% = 75%	Cost = N200 = 80%
Producer	Wholesaler	Retailer

The illustration above indicates that a product which cost the producer ₦120 to produce will subsequently be sold to the final consumer at ₦ 250.

Selling price Cost + Mark-up

Mark-up

Selling Price = Mark-up percentage

Fixed Mark-up percentage could also be pre-determined by an organization and could be calculated on unit cost of product.

3. **Demand–Oriented**

The marketing concept stresses the importance of the customer and a crucial point for focusing on the customer is that of determining price. The producer is better disposed to increase price and quantity when the demand is high. Thus in the figure below, price 1, that is, P1 is charged when quantity Q1 is supplied and so on.

Figure 21: Demand-Price Interaction

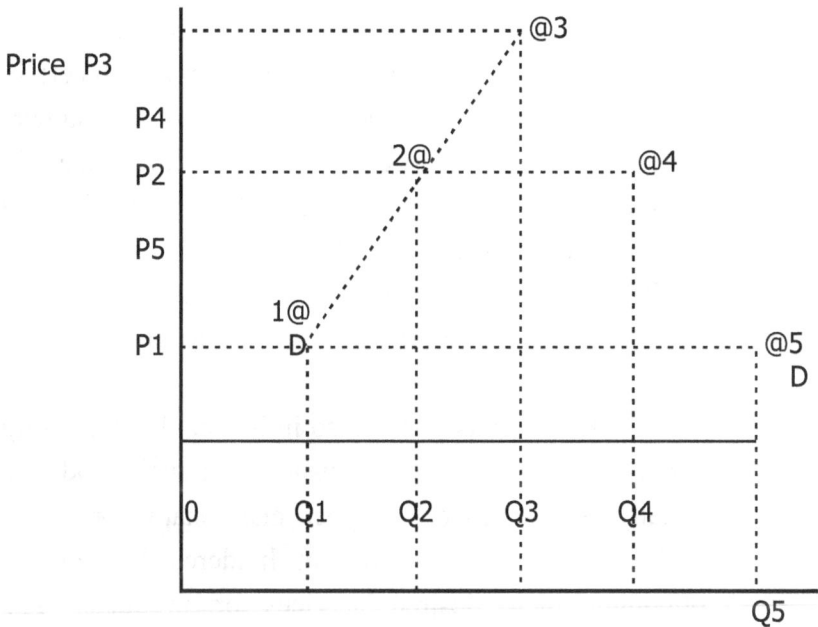

4.   Product Benefits

The degree to which the product will be beneficial to the consumer will affect the price he is willing to pay for it.

If the product is an essential one that the consumer must obtain then he will be willing to pay for it. This beneficial aspect of a product could be exploited by the producer to fix high price. For instance, the benefits to be derived from being educated compel educational consumers to invest all their resources such as energy, time, money to obtain it. Drugs have to be bought by patients in order to get well, doctors have to be paid for their services, lawyers too for litigations.

155

Essential parastatals that are monopolistic or oligopolistic can also influence price determination such as is being experienced presently in Nigeria with certain government prostates and corporations. Consumers have had to go through harrowing experiences in obtaining required services from the Power Holding Company of Nigeria (PHCN) Nigerian Postal Services (NIPOST); Nigerian Telecommunication (NITEL); public utilities, Passport, Corporate registration and the like.

Ostentatious goods also influence the marketing manager's pricing policy. Consumers of such goods are usually in the upper – upper class status or status seekers and therefore are not hindered by cost in obtaining their desired services or products. The products are usually custom made and tailored specifically to the need and taste of the consumers for which they are willing to pay for. These products, therefore, will command higher prices.

5.   **Consumer Target**

The consumer target will also influence the pricing policy of a product. There are circumstances where the same product will be priced differently depending on the target consumer. Variables that usually come to play are wealth, location, age, gender and perhaps literacy level. These discriminating prices are often exhibited when, for example, to watch a football match in the same stadium, state box side will attract a higher price than that of general side or you

156

hear of students or children(s) prices. High status income and sophisticated consumers are often charged higher prices than low-income ones. Location also plays a role in pricing, the same product can by priced differently in rural and urban areas. The same product would be sold cheaper in the open market than it would be in a super market or boutique.

6.   **Competitors**

Pricing is a highly delicate and technical task which tests the marketing managers capabilities. Marketing objectives, among others, are to create awareness, to ensure that adequate quantity of products are made available at the right place, right time and at a reasonable or fair price. The main issue then is, what is "fair price"? A price has to be fair to both the organization and the consumer. To the organization, products have to be sold to ensure adequate profit for the growth and sustenance of its entire operations while the consumer is interested in getting his money's worth in terms of benefits derivable from the utilization of the product.

But an organization does not exist in isolation, it is constantly influenced by its environment and the roles played by competitors cannot be over emphasized. The marketing manager aims at gaining and retaining product target market and, therefore, cannot afford to loose any fraction of it to rivals especially with products that have very close substitutes. Hence, there is a very inelastic range within which prices can be fixed in a particular industry, such as exists in drugs, detergents, drinks and petroleum industries.

Often a firm may decide to reduce its profit margin by pricing low in order to increase patronage. However, consumers' product perspectives should not be compromised especially in a highly competitive market in terms of product quality, branding, packaging and after sales services.

There is no rigid, right or ideal pricing technique, the technique or firm's pricing policy is often relative to so many variables such as the product internal and external environmental influences. At times two or more techniques could be adopted in determining product price.

CHAPTER 12

PERSONNEL MANAGEMENT

An organization may possess the best equipment, facilities, funds, goals and policies, but if the right calibre of staff is not available, very little of the set goals may be attained. Hence, the personnel manager has a vital role to play in staffing.

The Duties of the Personnel Manager include-

1. Recruitment of staff.
2. Interviewing and placement of successful applicants.
3. Wages and salaries negotiations.
4. Conducting induction course for staff newly employed.
5. Maintaining personnel records and statistics.
6. Grading and promotion of suitable staff, transferring, posting, disciplining, rewarding-such as in cash, kind bonuses, citations, plaques and welfare arrangements.
7. Keeping records and monitoring of government legislation concerning personnel matter for example Nigerian Income and Policy guidelines, minimum wages, salary scales, allowances, benefits, staff basic facilities – such as canteen, toilet facilities, health services, transportation, and healthy environment.
8. Organizing safety, health and welfare campaigns for employees.

9.   Refresher courses, workshops, seminars, lectures to update and enhance employees' performance.

Personnel responsibility defined importance of staffing manpower planning needs conditions of services.

Personnel Evaluation – Why Evaluate?

1.   For administrative decision making
2.   For the improvement of individual staff and organisational knowledge of weaknesses and strengths.

Process of Personnel Evaluation

a.   Setting of goals.
b.   Understanding set goals.
c.   Provide required supplies, facilities and enabling environment.

Attained results will point to the evaluation of set goals, and determine if modifications are required, determination of roles and performance and so the process continues, in a cyclic fashion.

Fig. 22:   **The Process of Personnel Evaluation**

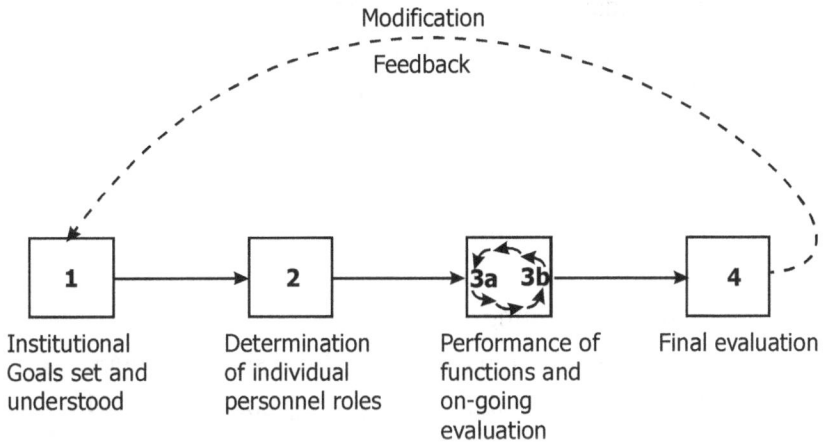

10.   **Industrial Relations:**   He should be in constant dialogue with workers and different unions to ensure that there is industrial peace and harmony. That there is cordial relationship between management and staff.

11.   **Counselling-** The personnel manager should ensure that there are no conflicts between organisational goals and those of the worker. Where there are, he should ensure that the worker is counselled and the areas of conflict resolved.

12.   Job evaluation, specification and description: All workers should be assigned their duties, responsibilities and authorities. They should be aware of what is expected of them on which they will thereafter be assessed or evaluated.

13.   **Health, Safety and Welfare of Employees:** There is apathy of employers towards employees health, safety and welfare in organisation.

161

In Nigeria, the Factory Act, 1956 makes provisions for minimum standard to be met by employers as regards workers; health, safety and welfare such as.

a. Clean environment.
b. Painting of office.
c. Toilet facilities.
d. Avoid overcrowding of workers.
e. Adequate ventilation.
f. Adequate lighting.
g. Solid construction of factory floor, stair, passages.
h. Danger signs in dangerous places, containers, and chemicals.
i. Fire extinguisher and other fire fighting equipment and workers should know how to operate them and where they are located.
j. Adequate exit doors.
k. Suitable drinking water containers and workers should have individual drinking cup.
l. Hand washing bowls with towels.
m. First aid box.
n. Canteen
o. Social and sporting facilities
p. Safety facilities
q. Cloakroom (dressing/changing room)
r. Staff bus
s. Housing
t. Pension schemes
u. Bonuses, loans for cars, houses or other needs..

Personnel Evaluation

Personnel Evaluation Techniques :

Sources of information for staff evaluation include-observation, records, bosses, colleagues subordinates, anstoners, performance. While evaluation techniques include appraisal/evaluation form, rating scale, written methods that is, by tests or examinations, multiple rating, committee rating, independent rating, management by objective (MBO) approach and self appraisal. Assessment of workers performance will be compared against set goals, after which appraisal results should be communicated to all concern.

Staff Recruitment and Training
Staff Recruitment

A major responsibility of the Personnel Manager is staff recruitment. He has to ensure that the right calibre and number of workers are available to work towards the attainment of organizational goals; and individual development.

Sources of Recruitment: There are two main sources of staff recruitment. They are external and internal.

Internal Recruitment:
By this method, vacant positions in the organisation are filled with already existing staff who are qualified. Members of staff are encouraged to apply if they meet the stated requirements for the position sought for. The usual process of recruitment will then be followed.

External Recruitment:
The personnel manager can also source for staff from outside the organisation. The procedure for external recruiting is more

complex than that of internal. The vacancies have to be publicized through the chosen medium or media and more applications are usually received for processing. After the vacant positions have been declared, the following steps will then be taken.

1.   *Advertising:* Newspapers, electronic media, bill-boards, recruitment agencies, friends and relations,
    -        Professional organisation.
    -        Schools and other educational establishments.
    -        Circulars and posters.

2.   *Procedures for Recruitment:* Screening applications (short-listing for interview).
     Test/interview (written, verbal or both, on the job testing or practical testing, for example typing speed, shorthand ability or computer proficiency to judge applicants appearance, poise, speech, traits and other characteristics.

3.   *Appointment decision:* Check references.

4.   *Appointment letter:* Indicating terms of employment, remunerations, job expectations or specifications.

5.   Placement.

6.   Induction programme.

Staff Training

This could be on-the-job or off-the-job or both. This has become necessary because of rapid technological advancement and sophistication. Superiors and peers are usually responsible for on-the-job training. But there are various types of off-the-job training such as:

a.   Vestible Training: Workers are trained in specific jobs in a special part of the organisation.

b.   Conference Method: Group-centred with a leader and information is gathered from discussions.

c.   Role-Playing: Trainees are made to play a particular role, especially of a superior and know how to handle situations if, there were really in that position, for example, if I were to be the General Manager, how will I handle this situation? or what will I do?

d.   Group discussion: Members of the group to discuss a particular problem and proffer solutions.

e.   Simulation method: Trainees act out a real situation to get acquitted with real life decision making.

f.   Special courses: Training undertaken in established educational institutions for specific trainings, such as in the Universities, Professional Schools, like Institute of Chartered Accountants of Nigeria (ICAN), Nigerian Institute of International Affairs (NIIA), Marketing, Public Relations, Computer, Law, Banking and Insurance.

g.   Case method Problem, facts of situations are presented to trainees and are required to study the situation, analyse, reason and present conclusions and recommendations.

h.   Sensitivity training: Trainees are placed in stress situations and are observed, to determine how sensitive they are to each other's feelings and problems. This will reveal if they are selfish, self-centred, individualistic or group unity and sensitivity.

These trainings are all geared towards attaining the appropriate workforce that will actualize the organizational goals, ensure individual growth and societal needs.

CHAPTER 13

INDUSTRIAL RELATIONS

Industrial relations constitute an important aspect of perssonnel administration. It deals with the promotion of industrial harmony at work through the use of machinery such as collective bargaining, grievance procedures, joint consultation and statutory channels.

The need for industrial harmony in the face of the growth of well enlightened workforce, hard economic conditions and technological break-through cannot be over-emphasized.

The industrial relations function ensures that such harmony is sustained. It monitors the state of workers-management relations and advises the organization and the government. It is also involved in negotiations with the labour unions to prevent or settle industrial disputes.

Collective Bargaining

Collective bargaining is defined by the International Labour Organization (ILO) as:

Negotiations about working conditions and terms of employment between an employer, a group of employers or more employers organizations, on the one hand, and one or

167

more representative workers' organizations on
the other with a view to reaching agreement.

Collective bargaining, therefore, has become an important mechanism for setting the procedures for the settlement of industrial disputes and also for resolving disputes when they inevitably occur. That is, it is a process in which representatives of two groups meet and attempt to negotiate an agreement that specifies the nature of future relationships between them.

There are two basic types of collective bargaining between workers and management.

1.   Traditional and

2.   Integrative

1.   Traditional bargaining is concerned with the distributions of benefits, such as wages, working conditions, promotions, management rights and so on.

Tactics of this include presenting demands, haggling, cajoling, presenting counter- offers and threatening strikes and lockouts.

2.   Integrative bargaining tends to grow out of stressful situation. The pressures placed on companies and unions by international competition have led to the giving back by the union of certain items gained through traditional bargaining. The management agreement stipulates that the firm would open its books and provide full disclosure of all pertinent information to the union; and create opportunities for union members to participate in decision-making processes and governing the workplace. This power sharing

168

approach is supplemented with an employee stock ownership or profit-sharing plan and a labour union representative can even be placed on the company's board of directors, thus, enabling him to receive all types of management information.

Union Bargaining Pressures

The labour union has certain strategies and tactics that it utilizes to extract greater concessions from the employer, such as, haggling, cajoling, and demanding more in the expectation of getting less. In addition to these manoeuvers there are certain stronger types of pressure that are sometimes used. These are:

1. Strikes
2. Picketing and
3. Secondary Boycott

1. **Strikes:** This is a concerted and temporary withholding of employee services from the employer for the purpose of extracting greater concessions in the employment relationship than the employer is willing to grant on the bargaining table.

It is defined in the Trade Disputes Act (1976) as:

The cessation of work by a body of persons employed acting in combination, or a concerted refusal or a refusal under a common understanding of any number of persons employed to continue to work for an employer in consequences of a dispute, done as a means of compelling their employer or any person or body of person employed, or to aid other workers in compelling their employer or any other person or body of persons employed, to accept or not to accept terms of employment and physical conditions of work.

Under the Trade Unions Act (1973) it is provided that one of the matters to be provided for in the rules is the condition that no member shall take part in a strike unless a majority of the members have in a secret ballot voted in favour of the strike.

The strike, therefore, is a temporary stoppage of work as the workers intend that, at its conclusion, they will return to their jobs and the employers themselves view the strike in the same light.

At common law, an employer is not under any obligation to pay his worker during the period of a strike. The Trade disputes (Amendment) Act 1977 provides that "where any worker takes part in a strike, he shall not be entitled to any wages or other remunerations for the period of the strike. This amendment was promulgated by government to ensure that strikes are contained in such a way as not to disrupt the economy of the country.

Strike is recognized in the Nigerian legal system, but its use is acceptable to the extent that it is properly used for the furtherance of legitimate union objectives. Strike becomes illegal in the following circumstances:

1. When it deviates from its proper objective of settling a trade dispute between employers and workers;

2. When the methods adopted for the conduct of the strike are contrary to public order, such as arson or assault. Those involved could be charge under the criminal code, and

3. When the means for the peaceful settlement of the disputes have been established by agreement or legislation, and the union fails to use these or embarks on a strike action without first exhausting those procedures.

Although Section 37 of the 1979 Constitution provides that membership of trade unions is the right of all citizens, there are, however, certain groups of person who are not allowed to go on strike because they are considered to be providing essential or sensitive services to the country. Hence, employee in the following bodies are forbidden by law to belong to a trade union and by implication not to go on strike.

(a) Members of all armed forces and the police.

(b) Employees in
    (i)   Prisons Department,
    (ii)   Customs Preventive Service.
    (iii) Nigerian Security Printing and Minting Company Limited.
    (iv)   The Central Bank of Nigeria.

(v)   The Nigerian External Telecommunications Limited.

(vi)   Employees in every Federal or State Government establishment where such employees are authorized to bear arms.

In the case of other essential services where trade unions are allowed, the workers are not to embark on strike until all the statutory machineries for the settlement of disputes have been exhausted.

These services include:

(a)   The Public Service of the Federation or of the State.

(b)   Any public authority connected with: electricity, water, fuel of any kind, sound broadcasting, postal, telegraphic, cable, wireless or telephone communications, ports, airports, transportation of persons, goods, liverstock by road, rail, sea, river or air, hospital and other health matters, or fighting.

In addition to the above, the Minister of Labour may from time to time, by order, specify any other establishment which in his view, should not entertain union activities.

There are various types of strikes. Among them are the following:

a.   *Recognition Strike:* This is a strike to force the employer to recognize and deal with the union.

172

b.   *Economic Strike:* This is the typical strike based on a demand for better wages, hour and working conditions than the employer is willing to grant.

c.   *Jurisdictional Strike:* This occurs when two unions argue about which one has jurisdiction over a type of work and attempt to exert pressure upon the employer to allocate it to one or the other. This strike is illegal as their employer is caught in the middle between the two warring unions.

d.   *Wildcat Strike:* This is a quick, sudden and unauthorized type of work stoppage. It is not approved by union leadership, it is viewed as a "fractional bargaining" by a subgroup of employees who have not achieved satisfaction through regular grievance processing or collective bargaining procedures.

e.   *Sit-down Strike:* This occurs when employees strike but remain at their jobs in the firm. This type of strike action is regarded as illegal since it constitutes an invasion of private property. Employees are free to strike for certain objectives, but they must physically withdraw from the firm's premises.

f.   *Sympathy Strike:* If other unions who are not party to the original strike consent to strike in sympathy with the original union, this is termed a "sympathy strike". It is an attempt to exert an indirect pressure upon the employer.

2.   **Picketing**

In picketing, the union desires to keep the firm completely closed during the strike. The strikers, usually carrying placards, chanting songs and solidarity slogans, patrol in front of the company entrance.

This is the most effective device for accomplishing their objectives.

If there is no direct confrontation by management, picketing will be routine and peaceful, but if management threatens the workers, then picketing can turn into violence as non-strikers are attacked, cars and other properties could be damaged.

3.   **Secondary Boycott**

A secondary boycott takes place when a union, which is seeking a concession from employer A, places pressure on other companies to influence employer A to grant the concession. The other companies will be pressurized to refuse to deal with employer A until their demands are met.

Preconditions for Collective Bargaining

The following preconditions should be recognized in any collective bargaining process:

1.   The parties must attain a sufficient degree of organization.
2.   They must possess the necessary skills to manage the intricacies of the bargaining process. Thus, a sufficient degree of literacy is essential.

174

3. They must be ready to enter into agreement with each other within the framework of the machinery establishment for the purpose: and

4. Collective agreements concluded must be observed by those to whom they apply.

Matters for negotiation at national level include the following;
Wages and Salaries.
Overtime rates (ordinary; Sunday, public holidays and rest days).
Hours of work
Annual leave
Leave allowance.
Sick benefits.
Out of station allowance.
Redundancy benefits.
Acting allowance.
Transfer/disturbance allowance
Maternity leave.
Housing allowance
Overnight traveling allowances.
Transport allowance.

Matters for discussion at organizational level include the following:
Method of production
Increased efficiency
Safety
Welfare
Training of workers

Disciplinary procedures

Bonuses

Scholarship awards

Long-service award

Compassionate/casual leave

Medical facilities

Death benefits

Shift allowance

Hazard allowance

Figure 15: Conceptual framework for the study of collective bargaining

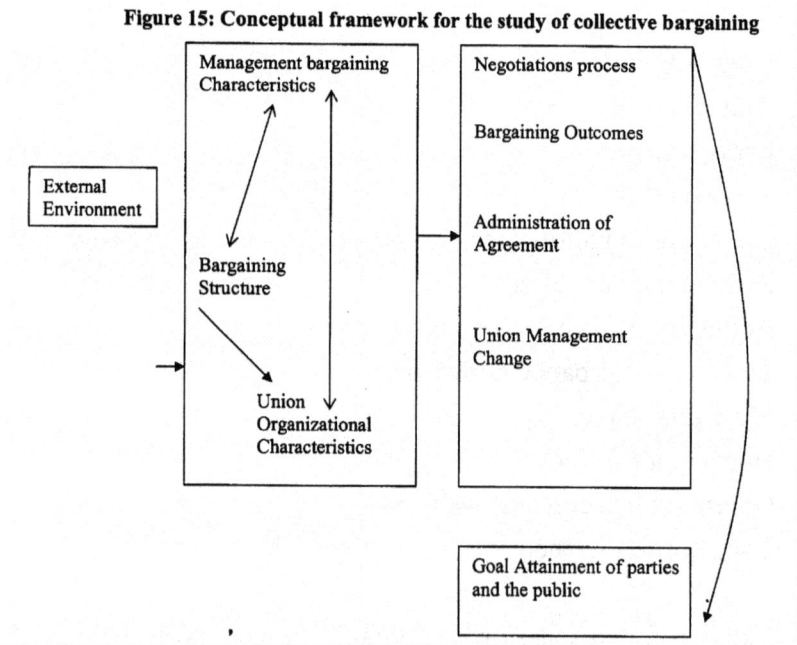

The explanatory variables in the framework are classified as characteristics of:

1. The union as a bargaining organization
2. Management as a bargaining organization.
3. The structure of bargaining and
4. The environmental context of bargaining

Figure 16: Simplified Macroeconomic model of collective bargaining

Marco
Economic
Polices

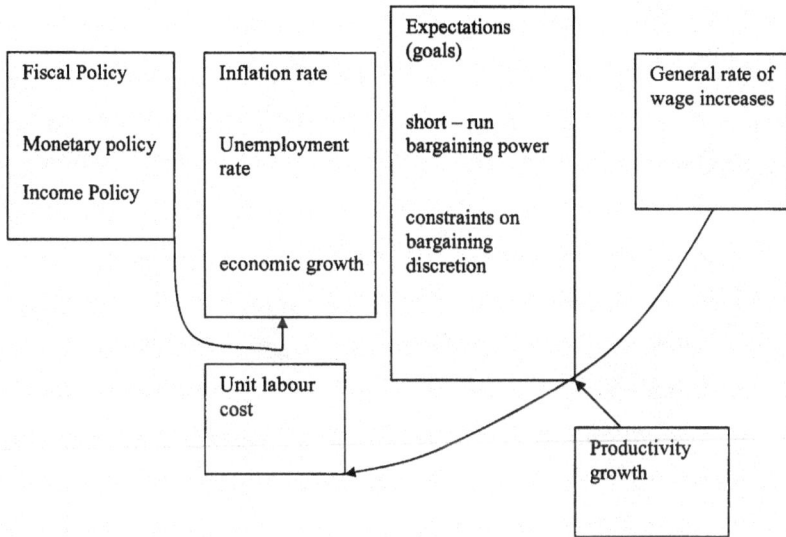

Fiscal Policy	Inflation rate	Expectations (goals)	General rate of wage increases
Monetary policy	Unemployment rate	short – run bargaining power	
Income Policy			
	economic growth	constraints on bargaining discretion	
	Unit labour cost		Productivity growth

Government constraints placed on the discretion of union and management negotiators.

Trade Unions

A trade union is defined in the Trade Unions Act 1973 as:

> *any combination of workers or employers, whether temporary or permanent, the purpose of which is to regulate the terms and conditions of employment of workers, whether the combination in question would or would*

177

not, apart form this Act, be an unlawful combination by reason of any of its purposes being in restraint of trade, and whether its purposes do or do not include the provision of benefits for its members.

The right to form or belong to a trade union is contained in section 38 of the constitution of Nigeria (1999). The section provides as follows:

Every person shall be entitled to assemble freely and associate with other persons, and in particular he may form or belong to any political party, trade union or any other association for the protection of his interest.

Functions of Trade Union

The functions of a trade union include the following:-

1.   Negotiation with management to improve the level of pay and conditions of work of its members

2.   Negotiation with management to protect the jobs of its members and to secure a good prospect of a prosperous future for them.
3.   Negotiations with management to improve physical conditions, health and safety at work
4.   Lobbying politicians to obtain legislation to improve conditions of work.

5. Encouraging political and social consciousness amongst its members, in the belief that political change might be necessary to improve the well-being of workers.

6. Developing political affiliation with other trade unions to create a "power base" for achieving political influence over government.

7. Attempting to become involved in management's planning functions and decision-making process. This might be achieved by means of joint consultative committees.

8. Provision of help and support to individual members who have the need for this. This help may arise from a particular incident or dispute at work in which a member is aggrieved by a particular management decision. On a more general level, a union might wish to provide financial support for the widows and orphans of members who have died or financial assistance to a member who is maimed through accident or ill- heath.

Management of Conflict

The process of integrating interest requires both preventive and curative activities. Despite the best of management practices in acting and communicating, conflicts between employees and management will occur. A total absence of conflict needs to be watched as it could indicate that such conflicts are being suppressed, like sitting on a keg of gunpowder that could explode unexpectedly.

Thus, the first step in the resolution of conflicts is their discovery and exposure, and management should create many upward communication channels that can bring dissatisfaction

179

to the surface. Credits can be given to management for recognition of the importance of good organizational morale and also to the growth of labour unions.

The following avenues are ways of discovering conflicts of interest.

1. **Grievance Procedure**

    This is the most important channel through which dissatisfaction could be communicated to management.

    Through this channel, the aggrieved or dissatisfied individual should have the courage to complain to the superior concerned and the issue discussed by both of them.

2. **Direct Observation**

    Not all grievances are expressed orally or written, but through numerous non- verbal behaviours. It is the responsibility of the superior to observe the behaviours of his subordinates and know when negative changes occur.

    An aggrieved worker can express his dissatisfaction in various ways, his productivity will deteriorate, he is withdrawn, highly resentful, irritable, and aggressive.

    Absenteeism and lateness also constitute symbols of protest and frustration.

    In addition to direct observation of subordinates behaviour, the study of various records and statistics can also give clues to general areas of trouble for instance, from the individual's personal records, it will be known when he was last promoted and whether he has received his promotions and increments as and at when due; he will also be compared with his colleagues to know if he has been treated equitably.

Examination of records and discussions with the worker's peers will also reveal more about his motives, such as, the rate of request for transfer, in-service training application not granted, number of queries received, disciplinary cases and the like. A good superior, therefore, needs to intervene to alleviate the subordinates problems if productivity is not to be adversely affected.

3.   **Suggestion Boxes**

These are boxes provided by management in strategic places in the organization because of its concern to bring all conflicts of interest to light. The aggrieved worker is, therefore, encouraged to submit his complaint in writing and dropped into the suggestion or complaint box.

The complainant may or may not identify himself, anonymity, however, will provide the coverage to submit a dissatisfaction uninhibited.

4.   **Open-door Policy**

Most top management officers usually announce that they operate an open-door policy, that is, any aggrieved person should freely come to their offices and discuss anything. But it is well known that, it is not easy getting in to see a top officers because of bureaucratic bottle-necks, gatekeepers or red tapism, such as, the supervisor, security men and secretaries.

A top officer who sincerely wants to operate an open door policy should make himself accessible by minimizing or removing obstacles.

5.   **Personnel Counsellors**

Some large organizations hire trained psychologists to act as counsellors for employees. The rationale for this, is that, employees may be reluctant to express their grievances to their superiors, so they then go to a neutral person, the counsellor, who will protect their identities and confidence.

6.   **Ombudsman**

An organization may operate a complaint office which workers can go to as last resort. The ombudsman or woman who is in-charge decides on which complaint to accept or reject. If he accepts the complaint, he will then investigate and make recommendations to the appropriate officer and even to the Chief Executive as he is regarded as an additional set of ears.

7.   **Exit Interview**

This takes place between manager and employee who has resigned. It is the last opportunity for the manager to know why the employee is resigning. This interview does not always yield the desired result as the employee is usually reluctant to discuss it. However, such employee is known after leaving the organization to open up and provide substantial and vital information as he no longer fears for poor reference letter or withholding of financial or other separation benefits.

8.   **Miscellaneous Channels**

Periodic questionnaires could be designed and distributed to employees to elicit responses to aspects of management policies that are regarded as not favourable or satisfactory to them. An open-ended question included will also give management an insight into employees' dispositions to work.

Group meetings could also be used or meet-the-workers' forum or questions and answers sessions. This will give workers and superiors an open opportunity to discuss issues that workers are dissatisfied with.

Collective bargaining, of course, is a veritable method of discovering conflicts of interest.

In extreme cases, some organizations employ informers or spies to interact with workers incognito and gather relevant information for management. This technique could be tolerable if management uses the information to better the lot of the workers, but could be objectionable if used to punish or sanction the workers.

Other techniques found by management to be effective could be adapted from time to time as situations vary from one organization to the other.

Statutory Procedure for Settling Trade Disputes

Trade disputes as defined by section 55 of the Trade Union Act of 1973 is the misunderstanding or disagreement between employers and workers, or between workers and workers, which is connected with employment or non-employment or terms of employment or conditions of work of any persons.

In effect, the three basic elements of the definition are:

i.   the subject matter of a trade dispute.

ii.   the parties to it.

iii.   the purpose.

In accordance with the Trade Dispute Act of 1976. There are laid down procedures for settling Trade Disputes. Where a trade dispute exists or is apprehended, the provision of the Act shall apply in relation to the dispute:

Step I: If there exist agreed means for settlement of the dispute voluntarily of the parties involved, they should explore that means first.

Step II: If the attempt to settle the dispute voluntarily fails or if no agreement of settlement is reached, the parties shall within seven days meet or send their representatives to a meeting under the presidency or a **mediator** mutually agreed upon with a view to the amicable settlement of the dispute.

Step III: If within fourteen days the mediator fails to settle the dispute, the dispute shall be reported to the Minister of Labour and Productivity. The report shall be in writing and shall record the points on which the parties disagree and describe the steps already taken by the parties to reach a settlement.

184

The Minister has three options:

a.   The appointment of a conciliator he thinks can yield some influence on both parties.

b.   A reference of the dispute for settlement to the Industrial Arbitration Panel (IAP) and the National Industrial Court (NIC).

c.   A reference of the dispute to a Board of Inquiry.

The Conciliator:

The conciliator shall inquire into the causes and circumstances of the dispute and by negotiation with the parties endeavour to bring about a settlement. If a settlement is reached within fourteen days of his appointment, the conciliator shall report to the Minister and present him with a memorandum of the terms of settlement signed by the representatives of the parties and as from that date, the terms recorded shall be binding on the employers and workers to whom those terms relate. If any person does any Act in breach of the terms, he shall be guilty of an offence and liable on conviction.

But if the conciliator after attempting negotiation with the parties and he is satisfied that he will not be able to bring about a settlement, he will report the fact to the Minister.

The Industrial Arbitration Panel:-

Within fourteen days of receiving the conciliators report of chilled negotiation, the Minister shall refer the dispute for settlement to the Industrial Arbitration Panel. The IAP composed of not less than twelve members includes two representatives for the interest of the employers and two persons representing the interests of the workers.

The IAP shall make its award within forty-two days or a period as specified by the Minister and send a copy to the Minister. If the Minister is not comfortable with some or all of the awards, he will refer the award back to the IAP for reconsideration; but if no objection, the award will be gazetted and shall be binding on the employers and workers to whom it relates any offender will be held liable.

It is worthy of note here that once the settlement process has commenced no employer should declare or take part in a lock out and no worker should take part in a strike – be it work-to-rule; sit-in or total strike.

If notice of objection to the award of the IAP is given to the Minister, he shall forthwith refer the dispute to the National Industrial Court. The award of the NIC shall be final and shall be binding on the employers and workers to whom it relates.

The NIC is composed of at least five members with the President who must be a judge of a court of unlimited jurisdiction in civil and criminal matters and a member who must have a competent knowledge of economics, industry or trade.

Boards of Inquiry:- Where any trade dispute exists or is apprehended the Minister may cause inquiry to be made into the causes and circumstances of the dispute and if he thinks fit, refers such dispute to a board of inquiry appointed for the purpose. The board shall inquire into the matter referred to it and report thereon to the Minister. The composition of the board could be one person or more depending on the decision of the Minister.

Under normal circumstances, that is, applicability of democratic principles, laws and procedures, the government will not prescribe a union without having followed due process as enumerated above. But in a military era where issues are handled with military fiat or precision, a decree can be promulgated that will amend or nullify an earlier one issued by the same authority. One may then continue to ask, is the gun mightier than the pen or is the pen mightier than the gun?

CHAPTER **14**

THEORIES OF MANAGEMENT

The history of management thinking must be studied with a clear idea about what it was primarily trying to achieve. Writers on management and organization hold the view that if certain principles of management and organization are put into practice, then the management will be more successful in ensuring that the objectives of the organization are achieved, and in an efficient manner. Their aim was (and still is) effectiveness and efficiency in the use of human and non-human resources to achieve organizational goals.

Early schools of thinking about this were:

a.   The classical and scientific management schools, and

b.   The human relations or behavioral school.

1.   Frederick   Winslow   Taylor   (1856–1915) acknowledged as the father of Scientific Management.

Taylor's famous work entitled The Principles of Scientific Management was published in 1911.

Scientific Management involves a complete mental revolution on the part of the worker engaged in any particular organization as to his duties towards his work, his fellow men and employer. And it involves the equally complete mental revolution on the part of those on the management's side – the foreman, superintendent, the general manger etc- toward their fellow workers in the management, workmen and all of their daily problems.

188

The fundamental principles that Taylor saw underlying the scientific approach to management are:

1. Replacing rules of thumb with science (organized knowledge).
2. Obtaining harmony in group action, rather than discord.
3. Achieving co-operation of human beings, rather than chaotic individualism.
4. Working for maximum output rather than restricted output.
5. Developing all workers to the fullest extent possible for their own and their company's highest prosperity.

In other words, Taylor argued that management should be based on well – recognized, clearly defined and fixed principles, instead of depending on more or less hazy ideas.

2. Elton Mayo and the Human Relations School (1880–1949)

In the 1920s, Elton Mayo joined a group who had undertaken a long-term investigation into the effect of worker fatigue on productivity and the possibility that rest periods would result in a rise in output, in this they were given a free hand by executives of the Hawthrone plant of the Western Electric Company in Chicago where the experiments were conducted.

The most famous of these Hawthrone experiments was the one concerned with the assembly of telephone relays, a repetitive operation performed by women. Since the job was manually done, output depended largely on the speed with which the operators worked.

A financial incentive was already in effect for the work. Five experienced workers were selected to take part in the experiment, with their own full knowledge and consent. Without their knowledge, however, a report was kept of each girl's production for weeks before any changes were made, this was done so as not to influence their rate of production.

1. The girls were given two rest periods, each five minutes long, for five weeks.
2. Each period increased to ten minutes each for a period of four weeks.
3. Six rest periods of five minutes each for a period of four weeks.
4. Two rest periods of ten minutes each, and the girls were served soup or coffee and a sandwich during the morning rest and something light in the afternoon. Since they often came to work without breakfast, it was felt that this might possibly stimulate their productivity.

And finally, in order to given them more time to eat, the morning rest was lengthened to fifteen minutes.

Schedule 4 was then continued for a period of months and various other changes in the working day were introduced.

During all this time, output of the group kept rising. It might have been concluded that rest periods in some form, particularly when accompanied by refreshments were highly conducive to productivity, and also shorter working day, but surprising results emerged when rest periods, refreshments and shorter working day were eliminated, output rose to a new high, then rest periods and refreshments were again introduced and output still rose higher.

The girls themselves had no clear explanation of why they worked so much faster, it had occurred spontaneously without the provision of extra pay. One conclusion possible from all this was that supervisory practices on the regular assembly floor were actually holding down output.

Mayo's eventual conclusion, covering employee relations and administration in general was that what he called the "rabble hypothesis" must be disregarded. This hypothesis is that workers in an organization are a disorganized rabble of individuals, each of whom is acting in his own self- interest as logically as he is able. Rather, work is a group activity and in present day society in which traditional groupings and ties have weakened, the work group is especially important.

3.   Henri Fayol (1841 - 1925

Pioneer of Modern Operational Management Theory. One of the most famous of the analyses of management itself is that made by Henri Fayol, regarded as the father of modern operational management theory. A French engineer, Fayol was chief executive of a large coal and steel company. As a mining engineer, he had become accustomed to working with principles and techniques that embodied scientific truth and decided to formulate a universal set of principles that could be used in all management situations. He emphasized, however, that he used the word "principle" only for convenience, and that his principles were not immutable laws but rules of thumb to be used as the occasion demanded.

Fayol defined the functions of administration as:

1.   To plan.
2.   To organize (both men and materials).

3.   To command- that is to tell subordinates what to do.

4.   To coordinate.

5.   To control.

Fayol's fourteen principles of management are:

1.   *Division of Work:* This is the specialization which economists consider necessary to efficiency in the use of labour. The manager or worker always on the same job acquires an ability, sureness and accuracy which increase their output.

2.   *Authority and Responsibility:* Fayol stressed that those who have authority to issue orders should be willing to accept responsibility for the consequence. Authority should be equal to responsibility, that is, if a man is responsible for the results of a given operation, he should be given enough authority to take the actions necessary to ensure success.

3.   *Discipline:* Seeing discipline as respect for agreements which are directed at achieving obedience, application, energy and the outward marks of respect is absolutely essential for the smooth running of an organization.

Experience and tact on the part of the manager are put to test in the choice and degree of sanctions to be used as remonstrance's, warnings, fines, suspensions, demotion or dismissal. Individuals and attendant circumstances must be taken into account. The best means of maintaining discipline, he said, are to have:

a.   Good superiors at all levels

b.   Agreements made with individual employee or a union should be clear and fair as possible.

c.   Penalties should be judiciously applied.

4.   *Unity of Command:* This means that employees or subordinates should receive orders from one superior only.

5.   *Unity of Direction:* There should be one head and one plan for a group of activities having the same objective.

6.   *Subordination of Individual Interest to General Interest:* The interest of one employee or group of employees should not prevail over that of the organization. Management should try and harmonize organizational and employee interest, but where there is a conflict, the organizational interest supercedes.

7.   *Remuneration:* Wages and salaries should be fair. They should depend both on circumstances such as cost of living general economic conditions, the demand for labour, the economic state of the business, and on the value of the employee.

Remunerations and methods of payment should be fair and afford the maximum possible satisfaction to employees and employer

8.   *Centralization:* Fayol refers to the extent to which authority is concentrated or dispersed. The question of centralization or decentralization is a simple question of proportion.

In small firms, where the manager gives directives to subordinates, there is absolute centralization, in large concerns, where a long scalar chain is interposed between managers and the lower grades, authority has to go through a series of intermediaries.

9. *Scalar chain:* This is a chain of superiors form the highest to the lowest ranks, which should not be departed from unless when absolutely necessary. Fayol advises that Gangplanks should be used to prevent the scalar chain of command from bogging action down.

10. *Order:* This means place for every thing and everything in its place, a place for every one and every one in his place, and the right man in the right place. This demands precise knowledge of the human requirements and resources of the organization and a constant balance between these requirements and resources.

11. *Equity:* Loyalty and devotion should be elicited from personnel by a combination of kindliness and justice on the part of managers when dealing with subordinates. That is, justice tempered with kindness.

12. *Stability of tenure of personnel:* Both managers and employees need time to learn their jobs, if they leave or are removed within a short period, the learning time has been wasted. Unnecessary staff turnover is the cause and the effect of bad management.

13. *Initiative:* Initiative is conceived of as thinking out and execution of a plan by subordinates. The manager must sacrifice his own vanity to encourage and inspire those under him to show initiative within the limits of respect for authority and for discipline. The plans and proposals made will contribute to success of the business and to employee morale.

14. *Esprit de Corps:* This is the principle that "in union there is strength", that everyone should work in a harmonious atmosphere emphasizing the need for teamwork and the importance of communication in obtaining it.

In concluding his discussion of these principles, Fayol observed that he had made no attempt to be exhaustive, but had tried only to describe those he had the most occasions to use.

4. Chester Barnard the Systems Approach to Operational Management

An organized enterprise does not exist in a vacuum. Rather. It is mutually dependent on its external environment; it is a part of a larger system such as the economic system, the industry to which it belongs, and society. Thus the enterprise receives inputs, transforms them, and exports the outputs to the environment as in the figure below.

Figure 25: Input–Output Model

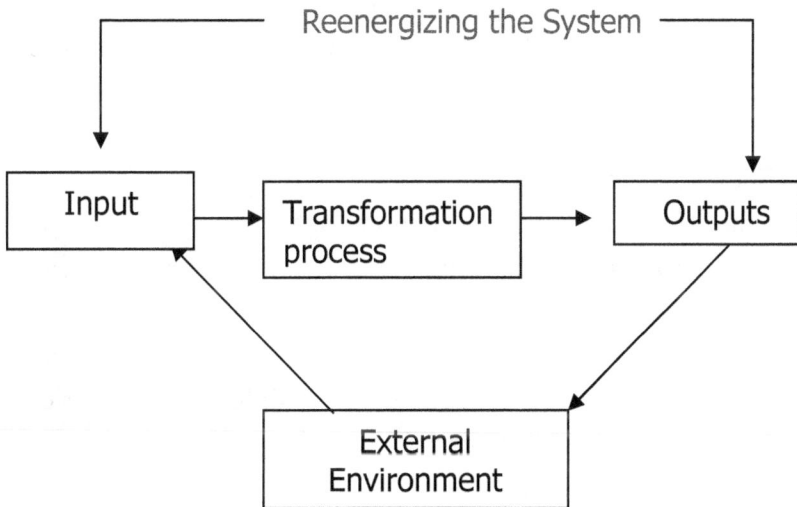

Inputs and Claimants

The inputs from the external environment as shown in figure 2 include people, capital, and managerial skills, as well as technical knowledge and skills. Unfortunately, many of the goals of these claimants are incongruent with each other, and it is the manager's job to reconcile these divergent needs and goals – such as those of employees, consumers, suppliers, stock holders, government, community, financial institutions, labour unions, even competitors.

Communication System

Communication pervades the total managerial process, it integrates the management functions, and it links the enterprise with its environment. Communication is essential in the selection, appraisal and training of managers. Also, effective leadership and the creation of an environment conducive to motivation depend on communication. It is through communication that one determines whether events and performance conform to plans or set goals.

The second function of the communication system is to link the enterprise with its external environment.

Reenergizing the System

Some of the outputs become inputs again:

- Satisfaction of employees becomes an important human input.
- Profits are reinvested in capital goods such as machinery and equipment, buildings, inventories of goods, tools and cash.

The Functions of the Manager

Planning: Selecting objectives and the strategies, policies, programmes, and procedures for achieving them is decision making, since it involves selecting from among alternatives.

Organizing: The establishment of an intentional structure of roles through determination of the activities required to achieve the goals of an enterprise and each part of it, the grouping of these activities, the assignment of such groups of activities to a manager, the delegation of authority to carry them out, and provision.

Figure 18: Systems Approach to Management

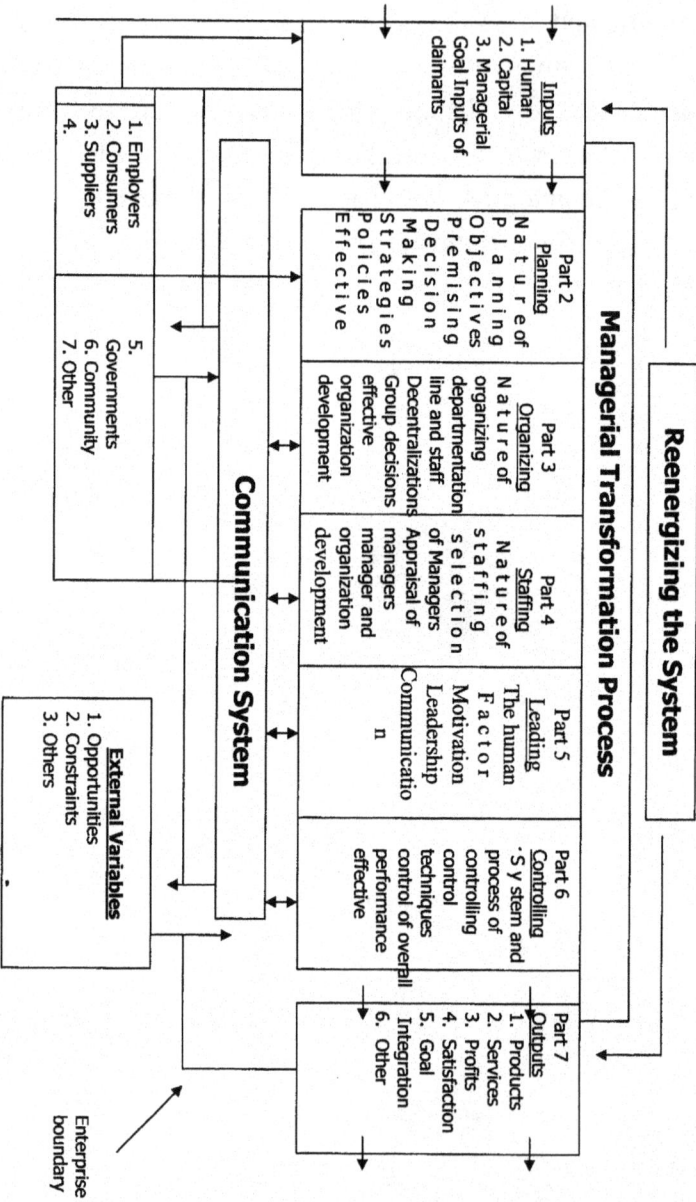

Reenergizing the System

Managerial Transformation Process

Inputs
1. Human
2. Capital
3. Managerial
Goal Inputs of claimants

Part 2
Planning
Nature of
Planning
Objectives
Premising
Decision
Making
Strategies
Policies
Effective

Part 3
Organizing
Nature of
organizing
departmentation
line and staff
Decentralizations
Group decisions
effective
organization
development

Part 4
Staffing
Nature of
staffing
selection
of Managers
Appraisal of
managers
manager and
organization
development

Part 5
Leading
The human
Factor
Motivation
Leadership
Communication

Part 6
Controlling
System and
process of
controlling
control
techniques
control of overall
performance
effective

Part 7
Outputs
1. Products
2. Services
3. Profits
4. Satisfaction
5. Goal Integration
6. Other

Communication System

1. Employers
2. Consumers
3. Suppliers
4.
5. Governments
6. Community
7. Other

External Variables
1. Opportunities
2. Constraints
3. Others

Enterprise boundary

need for effective managers also to be effective leaders. Since leadership implies follower ship, and people tend to follow those in whom they see a means of satisfying their own needs, wishes and desires, it is understandable that this area of management involves motivation, leadership styles and approaches and effective communications.

Controlling: Is the measuring and correction of activities of subordinates to assure that events conform to plan. Thus it measures performance against goals and plans, shows where negative deviation exist, and, by putting in motion actions to correct deviation, helps ensure accomplishment of plans. Although planning must precede controlling, plans are not self-achieving. The plan guides managers in use of resources to accomplish specific goals. Then activities are monitored to determine whether they conform to planned action.

Coordination: Is regarded as the essence of manager ship, for the achievement of harmony of individual efforts towards the accomplishment of group goals as the purpose of management. Each of the managerial functions is an exercise in coordination.

The necessity for synchronizing individual action arises out of differences in opinion as to how group goals can be reached or how individual and group objective can be harmonized.

Even in the case of a church or a fraternal organization, individuals often interpret similar interests in different ways, and their efforts toward mutual goals do not automatically mesh with the efforts of others. It thus becomes the central task of the manager to reconcile differences in approach, timing, effort, or interest and to harmonize cooperative and individual goals

5.   Management By Objective

When one discusses an organization's Management by Object (MBO), programme one may be referring to a number of practices. Terms used to describe MBO approaches include: management by result, work planning and review. Performance- planning evaluation, charter of accountability concept, individual goal setting, group goal setting, and participative goal setting. The exact name associated with objective setting has led to some of the confusion about what it involves, where it is implemented and how it has worked.

MBO is a logical extension of goal setting. However, much of the research supportive of management by objective came after years of implementation of the management by objectives process by hundreds of organizations. Management by objectives is usually credited to Peter Drucker (1954) who coined the phrase **Management By Objectives** and stressed the importance of setting measurable performance goals and appraising by results, which he argued should have a positive impact on employee motivation and performance. Credit is also given to Anthony Raja (1974) and to George Odiorne (1965) for popularizing an objective-oriented approach to managing. Since its inception management by objectives has achieved growing acceptance not only in business organizations but also in hospitals, government agencies and school systems.

While no definite prototype for management by objective programmes exists, all involve setting objectives in terms of expected results, working toward these objectives, and reviewing progress toward the objectives. The process, which

200

starts at the top management level, is an important part of the organization's strategic planning process.

The Management by Objectives process: Although there are many variations of Management by Objectives programmes, the process consists of **three phases**:

1. *Setting Objectives:* Superiors and subordinates establish, agree on, and state very precisely, preferably in writing, the specific results that are to be achieved within specified time lines.

2. *Developing Delivery Systems:* Strategies, activities, and processes are established to achieve the objectives. The end result is a delivery system that details precisely how individuals or building units will achieve the objectives.

3. *Examining Results:* At periodic times during the business year, results achieved by individuals or building units are compared to the objectives that were set.

The figure below depicts the three phases of management by objectives process.

Objectives are distinguished from business to business. In general, objectives have the following characteristics:

1. They are specific
2. They are challenging but realistic and attainable
3. They are measurable
4. They specify a time line for accomplishment.
5. They are accepted by business personnel or community.

Needs assessment concerns:

1. Strengths of the business goals and objectives.
2. Weaknesses
3. Strategic plans for the future

That is, needs assessment can be identified as discrepancies between what exists and what is desired, which represents a gap in performance of the organization when these discrepancies are determined, solutions through the fulfillment of management objectives can be developed for closing the gap.

Figure 19: The MBO Process

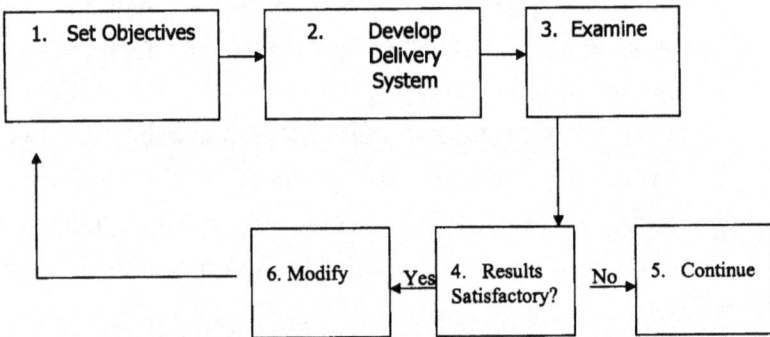

Figure 20: Relationship of Goals and Objectives in a Needs Assessment

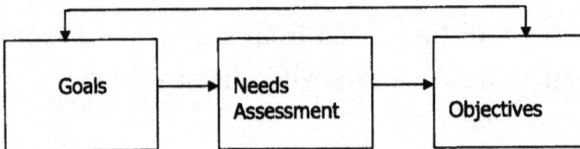

Figure 21:   Hierarchy of Objectives

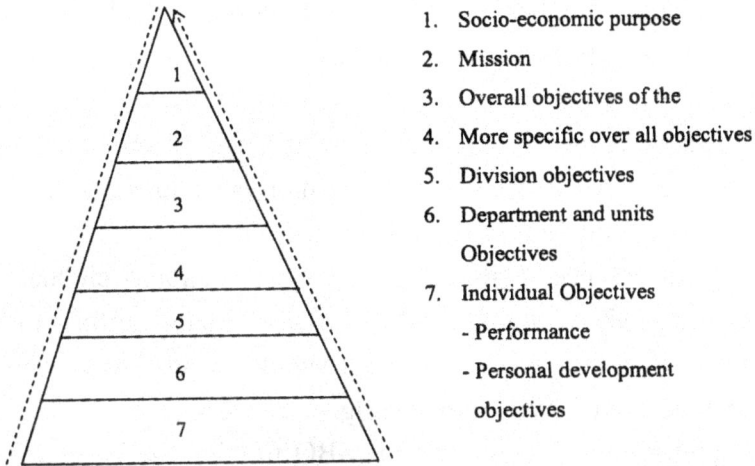

1. Socio-economic purpose
2. Mission
3. Overall objectives of the
4. More specific over all objectives
5. Division objectives
6. Department and units
    Objectives
7. Individual Objectives
    - Performance
    - Personal development
      objectives

job should be defined by the contribution he and his sales force have to make to the sales department, also the engineering department and others. This requires each manager to develop and set the objectives of his unit himself. Higher management must, however, reserve the power to approve or disapprove these objectives. But their development is part of a manager's responsibility. He suggests that Management by Objectives is a process that encourages managerial self-control. The manager is at the core of the process and he controls the   progress achieved in accomplishing worthwhile objectives.

Odiorne emphasizes a slightly different set of issues when he states that Management By Objectives is a process whereby the superior and subordinate managers of an organization jointly identify its common goals, defined each individual's major areas of responsibility in terms of the results expected of him, and use these measures as guides for operating the unit and assessing the contribution of each of its members.

The emphasis is the importance of mutual understanding between a superior and a subordinate. From both Drucker's and Odiorne's interpretations of Management By Objectives is the implication that through discussions and involvement a subordinate will be motivated to work harder and consequently improve performance.

In essence, MBO is an intervention approach that is concerned with initiating and stimulating better performance, among other things. It is, as Raja states, "a proactive" rather than a "reactive" style of managing.

The philosophical rudiments of MBO provide the bases for a process that includes a series of interrelated and interdependent steps.

Important Principles of Action

1. MBO requires the involvement of superiors and subordinates. The subordinates may be involved in a dyadic relationship, one superior one subordinate, or in a group arrangement of one superior and more than one subordinate.

2. MBO relies heavily on feedback, which needs to focus on result and should be as closely connected to behaviour and performance as possible.

3. The crucial first step in any MBO programme should be a thorough diagnosis of the job, the participants and the needs of the organization.

4.   The superior must be competent in counseling subordinates on the achieved results and the expected or agreed results for the next cycle.

Procedure for providing feedback and counseling
1.   The superior should create a trusting atmosphere and not focus on punitive factors.
2.   The superior should listen as much as possible.
3.   The superior should use reflective summaries to minimize misunderstandings
4.   The superior should encourage the subordinate to vent anger and disagreement.
5.   The superior should encourage the resolution of problems before the end of the counseling or feedback session.

Benefits of Management By Objectives
The advocates of MBO propose an attractive list of benefits that will accrue to an organization that implements MBO, some of these are:
1.   Increased short and long–range planning
2.   A procedure for monitoring work progress and results.
3.   Improved commitment to the organization because of increased motivation, loyalty and participation of employees.
4.   Improved clarity of a manger's job, organizational roles and structures.
5.   Increased communications between superiors and subordinates.

6. An improved organizational climate in general that encourages improvements in performance.

7. Helps develop effective controls by measuring activities and taking action to correct deviations from plans in order to assure desired accomplishment. Hence, there must be a clear set of verifiable guidelines.

Figure 22: An MBO Model For Superior–Subordinate Goal Setting

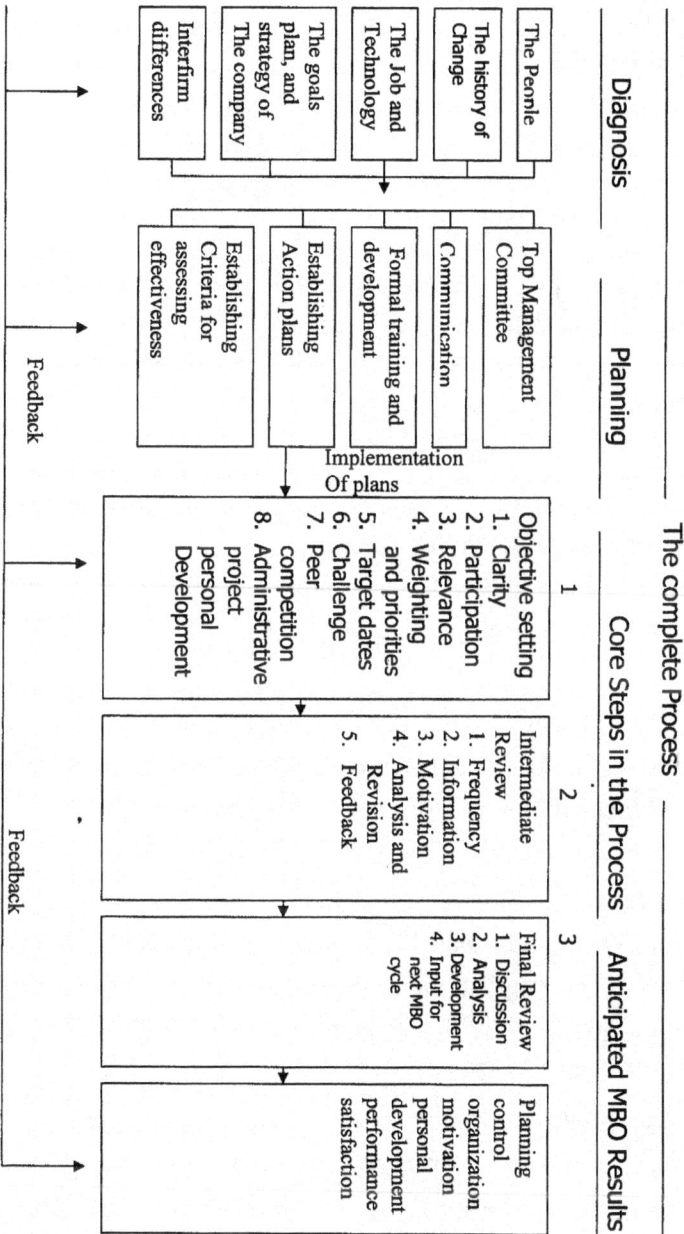

The complete Process

Core Steps in the Process

Diagnosis	Planning	1	2	3	Anticipated MBO Results
The Penple	Top Management Committee	Objective setting	Intermediate Review	Final Review	Planning control
The history of Change	Communication	1. Clarity	1. Frequency	1. Discussion	organization
The Job and Technology	Formal training and development	2. Participation	2. Information	2. Analysis	motivation
The goals plan, and strategy of The company	Establishing Action plans	3. Relevance	3. Motivation	3. Development	personal development
Interfirm differences	Establishing Criteria for assessing effectiveness	4. Weighting and priorities	4. Analysis and Revision	4. Input for next MBO cycle	performance
		5. Target dates	5. Feedback		satisfaction
		6. Challenge			
		7. Peer competition			
		8. Administrative project personal Development			

Implementation Of plans

Feedback

Feedback

Feedback

Weaknesses of Management by Objective

1.   Failure to teach the philosophy of how it works, why and benefits.
2.   Failure to give goal setters guidelines.
3.   Goals are difficult to set
4.   Goals tend to be short-lived or short-run.
5.   Dangers of inflexibility.
6.   Failure to harmonize goals, one person's objective may be inconsistent with another's
7.   Setting arbitrary goals.
8.   Failure to insist on verifiability, certain objectives may not be easy to appraise
9.   Use of generalized standards, that is, use of same appraisal standard for managers in all branches of an organization when local conditions are not the same. E.g. Managers in Lagos and Burutu.

Raja conducted two longitudinal studies of an MBO type programme at the Purex Corporation (USA). In his first study, production records, interview responses and questionnaire data from 112 managers were analysed. The data were collected after the implementation of the MBO programme. He found that productivity, which had been declining at a rate of 4% per month, was increasing at the rate of 3% per month after the MBO intervention. In addition, managers were more aware of the mission and goals of the organization, were more enthusiastic about evaluating and counseling subordinates, and believed that communications had improved since Management By Objectives was introduced.

In the second study, conducted four years later, Raja again collected data from seventy- four of the original participants. Productivity had continued to increase and also goal attainment. But got a number of complaints such as:

1.   The programme was being used as a whip.
2.   The programme increased the amount of paperwork.
3.   The programme failed to reach the lower managerial levels.
4.   There was an over emphasis on production.
5.   The programme failed to provide adequate incentives to improve performance.

In essence, these negative attitudes were viewed as indicators that despite some initial production improvements, other problems with the Management By Objectives programme existed.

Another study was carried out at Black and Decker (USA). The researchers interviewed participants and used attitude surveys.

The data analysis revealed that:

1.   Subordinates were more positive toward the programme as more difficult goals were set.
2.   Increased goal clarity, relevance, and importance resulted in more positive attitudes towards the programme and the interactions between superiors and subordinates.
3.   The more frequent the feedback sessions, the greater the subordinate's satisfaction, goal accomplishment, and relationship with the supervisor.

A second study at Black and Decker data analysis in which the interpretation was based on interviews and questionnaire responses, indicated that:

1. Managers now perceived Management By Objectives as a way of developing subordinates.
2. More managers believed that they had trouble with "personal improvement" goal setting with subordinates.
3. Satisfaction with Management By Objectives increased and there was an increase in the amount of work effort expended on goal setting.
4. There was no change in the amount of participation by subordinates in the goal setting process.

The researchers after reviewing their findings suggested that the most important factor in the successful implementation of Management by Objectives is top- management support.

As Odiorne notes, one of the major reasons for the failure of Management By Objectives in many organizations is that those in charge fail to recognize the potential character of the implementation process.

Management By Objections is indeed logical and systematic, but it must also deal with a number of factors, including power and authority, the organization form, and the value and expectations of people. For example, company 1: a Management By Objective programme was implemented by top management and company 2 the personnel manager implemented the programme. The power and authority highlighted by Odiorne was not equivalent in the two companies. The personnel unit had significantly less power and authority than did top management.

Key to Success with Management By Objectives

Management by Objectives and its associate approaches have been used for more than three decades. What have managers learned about its use and results? The following keys to success have been identified.

1. Top-Management Support, Commitment, and involvement is mandatory. Without it, Management By Objectives will not attain its set goals.

2. Management By Objectives should be **integrated** into normal, every day managerial activities. Managers must accept is as part of the management system, not just takes it on as a temporal process.

3. Management By Objective should emphasize **objectives or goals**, which, when attained, benefit both he organization and the individual manager. In other words, personal development goals must be included in any programme.

4. Resources (time and people) should be devoted to preliminary activities concerning **diagnosis and training**. A firm foundation of objective, plans for implementation, and trained personnel make later activities flow smoother.

5. Cognizance of **differences** in units, departments, and function is essential. Forcing a standardized programme on units that contain different methods, processes, and constraints may meet with resistance and possible failure. Slight modifications to a Management By Objectives programme at the unit level can prove to be quite valuable.

6.   Overemphasis on the development of **quantitative goals** will undermine success. Because managerial jobs are inherently ambiguous and difficult to evaluate and measure, qualitative goals are equally useful.

7.   A Management By Objective system should not generate too much paperwork. An effective programme can be run without the massive use of forms, memos, reports and so on.

8.   A great deal of emphasis should be placed on **evaluation**. Specific objectives of the Management By Objectives programme should be evaluated over time, either with internal or external agents.

9.   Overnight results should not be expected. Because of its complex nature and time frame, past experience has shown that concrete results probably will not be seen until about two years into the programme.

10. Finally, a **flexible and adaptable** Management By Objective system should be maintained. As the system is used, new and different factors are learned and evaluated.

Total Quality Management (TQM)

TQM is now widely acknowledged as an effective management tool for improving business performance, which in turn offers benefits to customers, employees and other stakeholders.

Many organizations that have applied the Total Quality Concepts into real performance improvements have recorded outstanding results. It has brought about visible changes in organizational culture, management style, technical innovativeness and interpersonal skills.

In other words, the key to on-going success through Total Quality is the effective implementation of processes that translate the concepts of Total Quality into real performance improvements.

For an organization to become a Total Quality one, it must achieve quality in everything it does; that is, all staff (security-men, cleaners, clerks, supervisors, managers, and Directors) should endeavour to achieve perfection in all activities or duties and at all times.

As society is becoming more enlightened and consumers more conscious of getting their monies worth, business organizations should, therefore, as a routine, appraise their numerous activities to determine if quality is lacking in any aspect.

For quality to be achieved in every aspect of a business, quality must be achieved in four component parts of the business; people, processes, products and service (3Ps 1s). Total Quality must be achieved in all four and not just in parts.

Figure 29: Total Quality key to Success

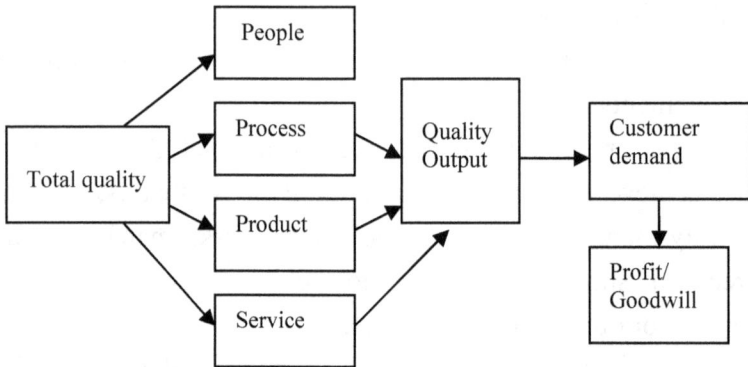

Quality People - These are highly motivated personnel of the organization, with appropriate skill, knowledge and ability to maximize the utilization of available resources, minimize wastage, effective and efficient use of time and subordinates to attain organizational goals. The staff must be satisfied with their respective jobs, be innovative, work in harmony in a conducive environment, respect constituted authority and be highly committed to the organization.

Quality Processes - These production processes are very vital to the survival and sustenance of the organization. The quality of the input and the conversion processes will determine the output. Quality of output will influence customer demand and hence organizations profit and good will.

Quality Product/Service

As earlier discussed, the organization has an unending duty to ensure the development of products and product lines and also services to satisfy the ever- changing desires of customers. This

214

involves developing quality products and rendering quality services which then can be made available in the right place, sold with the right promotion and price.

The Customer

Total Quality focuses on the customers. This necessitates the drive to provide goods and services that meet their needs and expectations. The customer may not always be right but he is always the boss of the organization. If the customer is not satisfied with the goods and services produced, his purchasing power cannot be converted.

What is Total Quality Management?

Total Quality Management can, therefore, be defined as the managerial ability or design of an organization to harness all available resources- man, machines, finance, processes, raw materials, expertise-to provide quality goods and services to meet the expectation of their customers at a reasonable price.

Quality, therefore, is viewed from the customers and not the organization's as customers are getting more conscious of their rights and getting value for their money. If a customer is not satisfied with the quality of goods and services been provided by a company, he will take his business to another company if it is not a monopolistic company. Business organizations should implement Total Quality Management (TQM) through a vision and conceptual plan, organizational plan, process design, and job design for staff. Keys to its success include partnership with other businesses staff development, recognition of internal customers high- level commitment, inclusion and participation of all stakeholders.

Benefits of Total Quality Management

1.   *Quality Management:* TQM leads to effective management of the organization because quality strategies and plans are designed for improving business performance, as quality is achieved in every aspect of the organization which in turn offers benefits to the customers, employees, shareholders, and other stakeholders.

2.   *Satisfied and Committed Employees*: When a company becomes a Total Quality company, it is expected that all its workers must endeavour to achieve quality in all their diverse duties and activities all the time. Hence, management should ensure that it's employees are highly motivated to work by providing quality working environment and conditions which in return will ensure job satisfaction and commitment of employees who will provide quality goods and services that will ensure continued existence of the organization and their job security.

3.   *Industrial Harmony:* A satisfied and committed employee is an invaluable asset to the organization as he fully identifies with the goals and objective of the organization. A total quality business, therefore, will experience minimal industrial dispute thus ensuring continuous production, minimal wastage and achieving industrial harmony.

4.   *Esprit de Corp:* A Total Quality company enjoys employee's teamwork. All employees relate to one another as partners in progress, thus ensuring effective

216

communication, cooperation and interaction among super ordinates, subordinates, and peers in both intra and inter-department.

5. *Increased Profitability:* A Total Quality Organization will produce quality goods and services at a reasonable or fair price. When customers are satisfied with the company's output, demand will increase, thereby necessitating increase in production, market share and profit.

6. *Competitive Advantage:* The provision of quality goods and services at fair price will ensure customer satisfaction. Quality companies, therefore, will enjoy increased market share and advantage over their competitors.

7. *Satisfied Customers*: The purpose of a business is to "create a customer and retain him". This is even more so for a Total Quality company. An effective strategy must be based on knowing what customers want. Do they want price, value, quality, availability, and service? When customer's needs and requirements are met at all times, then they will be satisfied and patronage will be ensured.

Problems of Total Quality Management

1. *High Cost:* To attain Total Quality in a business will require high capital and financial outlays as quality personnel will be required and trained. Highly technological machines, equipment and necessary gadgets will be acquired. Accurate planning must be

done as Total Quality is a one-time right process and not by trial-and-error.

2. *Fluctuating Customer Requirements:* Since Total Quality means continually satisfying customer requirements at minimal cost, management and production processes will have to be constantly adapted to suit customer's ever-changing needs.

3. *Delayed Production:* The most important factor for success of a Total Quality organization is meeting the customer's requirements which are ever- changing and adapting to varied needs could cause delay in production.

CHAPTER 15

ORGANIZATIONAL STRUCTURE

Max Weber, most influential of the structuralist founders, was very concerned with the distribution of power among the organisational positions in the bureaucratic structure.

Organizations, which Weber referred to as bureaucracies, set norms and need to enforce them; they have rules and regulations and issue orders, which must be obeyed if the organization is to function effectively. The organization can use some of its resources to reward those who follow its rulings and to penalize those who do not. Such discipline does not require the recipient (worker) of the order to agree with it, and if he accepts it as morally justified, he may obey the order.

1. To avoid punishment, disgrace
2. To avoid loss of money and/or prestige
3. To increase his income and/or status

The organisation can also maintain discipline by manipulating various rewards and sanctions in order to ensure maximum contentment and minimize disappointment.

The exercise of power, however, has major limitations.

1. It keeps the subject alienated even though he conforms.
2. He conforms by ulterior motives.
3. His conformity is likely to be limited to the matters explicitly backed by power.

4.   He will be unlikely to volunteer information, show initiative, or cooperate, except when he is explicitly forced to.

5.   In moments of crisis when the power structure of the organization weakens, he will tend to prefer other norms rather than that of the organization.

But when the power is legitimate that is, when the orders are issued or rules set conform to the values to which the subjects are committed – compliance will be much deeper and more effective. The subject will "internalize" the rules; he will find the discipline less alienating and identify with the organization.

It does not increase the material interest of the subordinate in compliance, it does not make the order or rule pleasant, but compliance fulfills a third kind of need, that is, the need to follow norms which match rather than conflict with one's values. In order to emphasize the difference between normative satisfaction of the need for justice (or legitimacy).

It is important to note, however, that some legitimate orders are gratifying, others may be legitimate and not gratifying, yet others can be illegitimate and gratifying.

Thus, Weber's study of legitimation introduces a whole new dimension to the study of organisational discipline. He used power to refer to the ability to induce acceptance of orders; Legitimation to refer to the acceptance of the exercise of power by it as in line with values held by the subject; and Authority to refer to the combination of the two that is, the power that is viewed as legitimate.

Weber's Typology of Authority

1. Traditional Authority – subordinate accepts orders of superiors by "that's how things are always done."
2. Rational – legal or bureaucratic authority. It agrees with a set of abstract rules which are legitimate.
3. Charismatic Authority – accepts orders as justified by or the influence of his personality with which they identify.

Weber suggested that to be effective and efficient as an organisational instrument, a modern organisational structure requires bureaucratic authority because it

1. has systematic division of labour
2. has specialization
3. has stability
4. allows the rationality of the production or administrative process to exert itself.

The Bureaucratic Structure Features

They all specify what makes a highly rational structure.

1. **Rules**: A continuous organisation of official functions bound by rules. Rules save effort of having to derive new solutions to various problems/cases; they facilitate standardization and objectivity equality in the treatment of many cases.
2. **Specific Sphere of Competence**: This involves
    a. Division of labour – sphere of obligations to perform functions.
    b. Authority to carry out these functions.

      c.   Necessary means and resources made available subject to definite conditions of usage. Not only must each participant know his job, have the means to carry it out, including the ability to command others, but must know the limit of his job, rights and power so as not to infringe or trespass to other participants' domains.

3. **Principle of Hierarchy**: The organisation of offices follows the principle of hierarchy, that is, each lower office is under the control and supervision of a higher one. There must be rules and regulations to guide compliance which must be systematically checked and reinforced.

4. **Technical Rules or Norms**: Weber feels that the root of the authority of the bureaucrat is his specialized and technical training and knowledge. It is on these bases that legitimation is granted to him.

5. **Segregation of Official and Personal Properties**: It is a matter of principles that the members of the administrative staff should be completely separated from ownership of the means of production or administration. Segregation of properties, and other elements of the status, such as residence and cars, to prevent misuse.

6. **Flexibility of Resources**: In order to enhance organization's freedom, the resources of the organization have to be free from external control, and positions cannot be monopolize by any incumbent, personnel/other resources should be allocated and reallocated as the need arises.

7. **Transactions must be in Writing and Documented**: Administrative acts, decision, rules and regulations are formulated and recorded in writing, critics view this as cumbersome, unnecessary and refer to it as "red-tapism." But Weber stressed the need to maintain a systematic record of norms and enforcement of rules which should be properly communicated to all concern in writing.

Workers should be compensated by salaries and other fringe benefits, so that they do not look up to clients for gratification, thereby, maintaining complete allegiance to the organization.

Non-Bureaucratic Head

Although the bureaucratic follow the rules the heads set them. The administrative body sets the organizational goals, but the heads decide which goals are to be served. Although bureaucrats are appointed, the heads are often elected or inherit the position, for example, presidents, cabinet members, boards of trustees, kings, heir, are typical non-bureaucratic heads of bureaucratic organisations.

Classification of Means of Control

There are three main categories: physical, material or symbolic,

1. Physical secures coercive power through the use of a gun, whip, imprisonment or other actions that hurt the body.

2. Material rewards – goods and services, money constitutes utilitarian power.

3.   Pure symbols: normative symbols prestige, esteem social symbols, love and acceptance. The use of symbolic control constitutes normative, normative-social or social power.

Line and Staff Relationship

A more precise and logically valid concept of line and staff is that they are simply in matters of relationship. In line authority, one finds a superior with a line of authority running down the line to a subordinate.

This gradation of authority is found in all organisations as an uninterrupted scale or series of steps. Hence, this hierarchical arrangement has been referred to as the scalar principle in organisation. The clearer the line of authority from the ultimate authority of management in an organisation to every subordinate position, the more effective will be the decision making and organised communication.

In many big organisations the steps are long and complex, even in small ones, the scalar principle still applies.

The nature of the line authority, therefore, highlights the relationship in which a superior exercises direct supervision over a subordinate.

The nature of the staff relationship is advisory, as staff is auxiliary. He is the professional, specialist or expert employed to assist the line officer.

The structure of organization is single track only, the staff function must adhere to the line in some dependent relationship.

Figure 30: Line – Staff Relationship

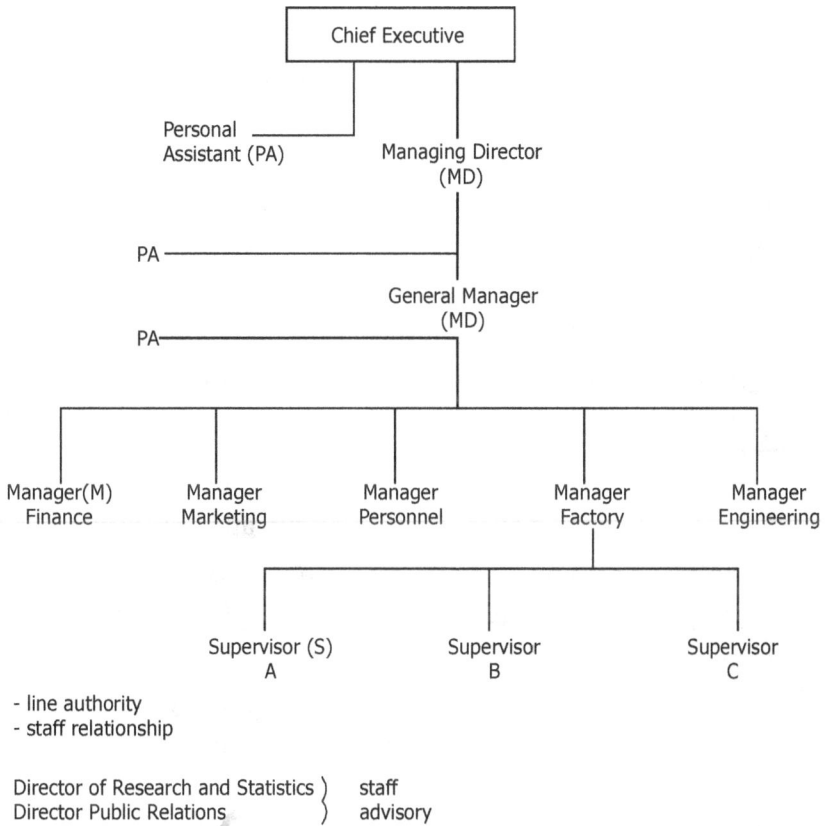

Chief Executive

Personal Assistant (PA)

Managing Director (MD)

PA

General Manager (MD)

PA

Manager(M) Finance	Manager Marketing	Manager Personnel	Manager Factory	Manager Engineering

Supervisor (S) A   Supervisor B   Supervisor C

- line authority
- staff relationship

Director of Research and Statistics) staff
Director Public Relations   ) advisory

Functional Authority is the right given to staff personnel which an individual or department may have delegated to him, over specified processes, practices, policies, or other matters relating to activities undertaken by personnel in departments, other than their own. This is done for numerous reasons, such as, lack of special knowledge and lack of ability to supervise processes.

Line manager will be deprived of this limited authority by their common superior to a staff specialist or another manager whose functions are now criss-crossing.

Figure 31: Line – Functional Relationship

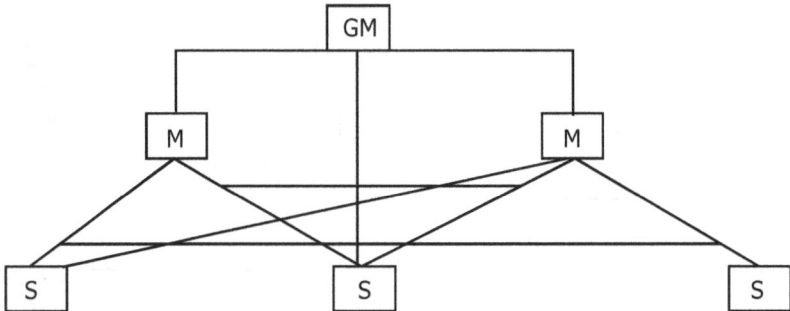

There is, however, lack of clarification in practice of responsibilities and authority, hence there is confusion compounded by ambiguity, lack of careful meaning and understanding and the unsurprising tendency of specialists to see everything in a company through their own eyes. There are varying perceptions of their authority as between themselves and their staff, their superior, and the various areas of the company subject to their influence.

Studies have shown the extensiveness of this lack of clarity and the conflict it engenders.

Thus, the best means of avoiding some of the problems, confusions, and frictions of functional authority is to make sure that responsibilities are clarified.

Limitations of Using Staff

1. **Danger of Undermining Line Authority**: The proposals of the staff specialists are received with enthusiasm by the company president and the departmental manager is expected to put them into effect.

2. **Lack of Responsibility of Staff**: In situations where the proposals are not successfully executed, the staff will accuse the manager of ineptness, lack of interest and sabotage, while the manager will claim that it was a poor plan hatched by inexperienced and impractical theories.

3. **Thinking in a Vacuum**: Proposals by staff specialist may not be practicable.

4. **Management Complication**: The directions of responsibilities and authorities may be so complex that management might end up spending valuable time straightening twisted lines of authority at the expense of more important issues.

5. **Making Staff Work**: Inefficiency may abound, which will now require high managerial skill, patient teaching of personnel and careful attention to principles of solve.

CHAPTER **16**

CONSUMER EDUCATION

Consumers have fallen victims of the devious manipulations of product and service providers, ranging from inadequate measurement scales, alteration of expiration dates, re-packaging expired drugs, fake items, substandard items, over-pricing, unsatisfactory services, to outright dumping, maiming and even killing.

They are also exposed to toxic, nuclear and other industrial wastes, poor sewage management and air, water pollutions.

Why Does the Consumer Need to be Protected?

The consumer, we now know, is the final user of a product and/or service. From numerous information available from personal experiences, media reports, court cases, human rights activists reports and others; we are made aware of the diverse methods applied by manufacturers, distributors, salesmen and women to provide adulterated and substandard goods and services to the consumer. Consumers buy adulterated and expired goods, drinks and drugs; they are also victims of fake measuring scales, mal-functioning equipment and many other dubious devices employed by sellers to dupe buyers, so as to "maximize" their "profits".

Consumers are normally expected to be vigilant and conscious of the state of the goods and services been offered to them, so as not to become victims of misleading advertisements about products/services, inadequate information on usage, side effects, unfavourable hidden clauses in contracts and other business transactions, unethical selling practices, questionable marketing practices, consumer gullibility and economic illiteracy. But the consumer is the boss. So, how do we restore consumer sovereignty in the market? These led to consumer movements and consumerists. But occasions do arise when sellers will out-smart them. When such situations arise, what can the consumers do? It is in recognition of these unfair deals received by consumers, that responsible governments and non-governmental bodies deemed it fit to establish bodies that would help to protect the consumers.

Consumer Education, therefore, can be said to be the concerted efforts of concerned government and non-governmental bodies to protect the consumer from all these unhealthy practices by informing them appropriately.

Some of these measures are preventive as they help to create awareness of possible sources and methods of harm to the consumer; while others are curative and compensatory.

Consumer Education and Protection Agencies

These are some of the bodies both governmental and non-governmental established to protect the interest of the consumers.

1. Standards Organization of Nigeria (SON)
2. Consumer Education and Protection Council of Nigeria (CEPCON)
3. Federal Environmental Protection Agency (FEPA)
4. Consumer Affairs Department

5.   Manufacturers' Association of Nigeria (MAN)
6.   Price Control Boards (PCB)
7.   Professional Bodies such as:
      (a)   Nigerian Medical Association (NMA)
      (b)   Nigerian Bar Association (NBA)
      (c)   Institute of Chartered Accountants of Nigeria (ICAN)
      (d)   Association of National Accountants of Nigeria (ANAN)
      (e)   Nigeria Insurers Association (NIA)
      (f)   Bank Directors Association of Nigeria (BDAN)
      These bodies are mostly associated with the service industry; and they regulate the conducts of their members and sanction erring members.
8.   Nigerian Association of Chambers Commerce, Industry, Mines and Agriculture (NACCIMA)
9.   National Drug Law Enforcement Agency (NDLEA)
10.   National Agency for Food and Drug Administration and Control (NAFDAC)
11.   Food and Drug Administration (FDA)
12.   Public Complaints Commission (PCC)

Consumer Responsibilities

Consumers are expected to:
1.   Be well informed about the product or service they intend to purchase.
2.   Do window-shopping and sampling.
3.   Examine product carefully and thoroughly.
4.   Check expiration dates on items, especially edible ones.

230

5. Be very vigilant of the activities of the seller, especially during measurement or packaging.
6. Collect receipts where possible.
7. Be weary of hawkers as they may not be easily identified or located in cases of default.
8. Seek redress with appropriate agencies.
9. Check NAFDAC number or the Nigerian Industrial Standard Mark (NIS) on relevant products.
10. Cautiously adher to advertisements, as they could be deceptive and fraudulent.
11. Adher meticulously to instructions or directives on usage/storage/ preservation of items especially for drugs and edible products.
12. Make fair and rational demands within existing legislation and standards.
13. Consumers should be honest and should not make frivolous accusations about products and services received.

Rights of the Consumer

Rights of the consumer are stated as follows according to the Consumer Education and Protection Council of Nigeria.

1. The right to safety
2. The right to be heard
3. The right to consumer education
4. The right to be informed
5. The right to choose
6. The right to redress
7. The right to a healthy environment

8.　　The right to get value for money spent

9.　　The right to the good things of life or the right to basic needs.

Enforceability of these Rights

In law, the consumer has the right to remedy or seek redress for an infringement of his right. As the general law maxim states, "where there is a right, there is a remedy".

Food: The quality, cost and marketing of food have been of prime interest to the government. The composition of the food content, especially the additives is specially monitored and this has led to the banning of many food contents and additives. For instance, of recent, there is the focus on bread, which is a staple food of most Nigerians. Certain additives have been banned and bakers have been warned of the penalties for defaulters and through regular jingles on television and other mass media, consumers are made aware of the inherent dangers of such additives.

There is also the situation of outright banning of the food items, such as imported chicken and turkey, that the Federal Government has banned because of the preservatives been used by the exporting countries. Drinks and cigarettes are not left out in this campaign for quality products such as banning of numerous fruit drinks, cigarettes and the government insisting that smokers should be warned that cigarette smoking is dangerous to their health and reduces life span.

Government has also had cause to set up a price control board, to regulate the cost of products and presently, the focus is on the price of petroleum products such as fuel, cooking gas, diesel and kerosene as they affect cost of transportation and preparation of food items and hence, cost of purchase.

Marketing of food items has also been of paramount interest as exposed food could be contaminated and thus, harmful for consumption. Storage facilities, especially for meat products, are also sources of concern.

Advertising: Through this technique, consumers are usually misled and exploited. Manufactures and sellers aim at arousing the desire of the innocent consumers to buy their products and services. Such advertisements on television, radio, bill-boards, handbills and other media, mislead consumers as to believe that their products provide numerous benefits to them. Such outrageous claims about products have, for instance, necessitated the ban on advertisements by traditional medicine "doctors" who will claim that their drugs can heal numerous ailments.

Standards Organization of Nigeria (SON)

The general expectation of every consumer is that the manufacturer or supplier of the product or service on demand should ensure that consumers' desires are placed above every other interests or else the product would be worthless.

The onus lies on the manufacturer or supplier to ensure that quality goods and services are provided.

Reasons for Establishing SON
1.   To administer standardization

2.   To ensure that manufacturers/producers are monitored to provide consumers the best of products/services at reasonable prices.

3.   To check the quality of goods and services produced within the country and those imported; with the overall aim of facilitating business transactions and engender economic development.

4.   To ensure fair trade practices and competition by the industry and provide common technical language in the industry.

5.   To enhance consumer confidence in products and services and facilitate sustainable economic development.

6.   To provide the necessary legal framework and environment.

7.   To ensure effective administration of such laws, acts and regulatory instruments with a view to ensuring that failures in quality control and production ethics are properly addressed.

These are typical functions of such regulatory agencies set-up to protect the consumers.

CHAPTER17

FINANCIAL BUSINESS GUIDELINES

A businessman who wishes to be successful should not run the affairs of his business haphazardly or by rule of thumb, but must plan and execute his decisions in a manner that will lead to efficiency, profitability and growth of his business. His decisions and actions must be based on accurate calculations derived from the utilization of relevant business information and data.

The following are relevant financial guidelines that will be of useful importance to a businessman.

Balance Sheet

The Balance Sheet is one of the most important accounting statements because it reveals the overall financial position of a business. It discloses the assets, liabilities and owner's capital or equity as at a particular date using data from accounting records especially the Trading and Profit and Loss Accounts. Unlike the Trading and Profit and Loss Accounts, the Balance Sheet is not a ledger account but a statement of assets, liabilities and capital.

Assets: These are things of value owned by a business and are classified as fixed and current assets. Fixed assets are those of long-term nature such as buildings, land, plant machines, vehicles, fixtures and fittings while current assets are of short-term nature such as stock, cash in hand and at bank, prepaid liabilities and debtors.

Assets = Capital + Liabilities

Liabilities: These are amounts owed by a business and are classified into long-term and short-term liabilities. Long-term liabilities as the name implies are debts that are to be repaid over a long period, usually more than a year such as loan, mortgage, hire-purchase. While short-term liabilities are prepaid income, creditors, bank overdrafts, salaries, interest and rent in arrears.

Liabilities = Assets – Capital

Capital: Is the excess of assets over liabilities and is considered the owner's equity.

Capital = Assets – Liabilities

Working example:

Ruby Nigerian Ventures
Balance Sheet as at November 22, 1999

Liabilities Capital	Assets Fixed Assets			
Balance 23/11/98	Land	490,000		
9,200,000	Building	1,500,000		
Add Net Profit 1,700,000	Fixtures & Fitting	390,000		
9,900,000	Vehicles	2,800,000		
Less Drawings 800,000	Machineries	3,400,000		
9,100,000	Less Depreciation			8,580,000
Long-term liabilities	**Current Assets**			
Mortgage 100,000	Stock 22/11/99		435,000	
Bank loan 200,000	Debtors			
Current liabilities	Less Provision for Bad Debts		80,500	
Bills payable 64,000	Bills Prepaid		5,500	
Creditors 50,500	Cash at Bank		425,000	
Bank overdraft 36,500	Cash in Hand		25,000	971,000
9,551,000				**9,551,000**

Working Capital: Working capital is the amount left to meet recurrent everyday transactions of the business after fixed assets have been purchased. A businessman should not over-capitalize at the expense of not having enough working capital because he will need to buy raw materials if it is a manufacturing outfit or finished goods for a trading outfit. It will also need to meet daily business expenses, pay salaries and bills.

Working Capital = Current Assets – Current Liabilities from the Balance Sheet or Ruby Nigerian Ventures working capital is 971,000 – 151,000 = 820,000.

237

Working Capital Ratio: Working capital ratio is very important to a businessman as it portrays the solvency or insolvency of a business. A minimum or equilibrium ratio should be 1:1 of current assets to current liabilities.

Working Capital Ratio $\quad = \quad$ $\dfrac{\text{Current Assets}}{\text{Current Liabilities}}$

$\qquad\qquad\qquad = \quad \dfrac{971,000}{151,000} = 6.4$ times

i.e. 6:1

This is a very solvent business.

Liquid Capital Ratio $\quad = \quad$ $\dfrac{\text{Current Assets} - \text{Stock}}{\text{Current Liabilities}}$

Gross Profit Sales (Net Turnover) – Cost of Sales

Gross Profit Percentage $\quad = \quad$ $\dfrac{\text{Gross Profit} \times 10}{\text{Sales}}$

Net Profit Percentage $= \quad$ $\dfrac{\text{Cost of Stock Sold}}{\text{Average Stock at Cost Price}}$

Or

$\qquad\qquad\qquad = \quad$ $\dfrac{\text{Net Turnover}}{\text{Average Stock at Selling Price}}$

Return on Capital Invested $\quad = \quad$ $\dfrac{\text{Net Profit} \times 100}{\text{Beginning Capital}}$

238

UNIT 18

COMPUTER TIT BITS

Window ME (Millennium Edition)

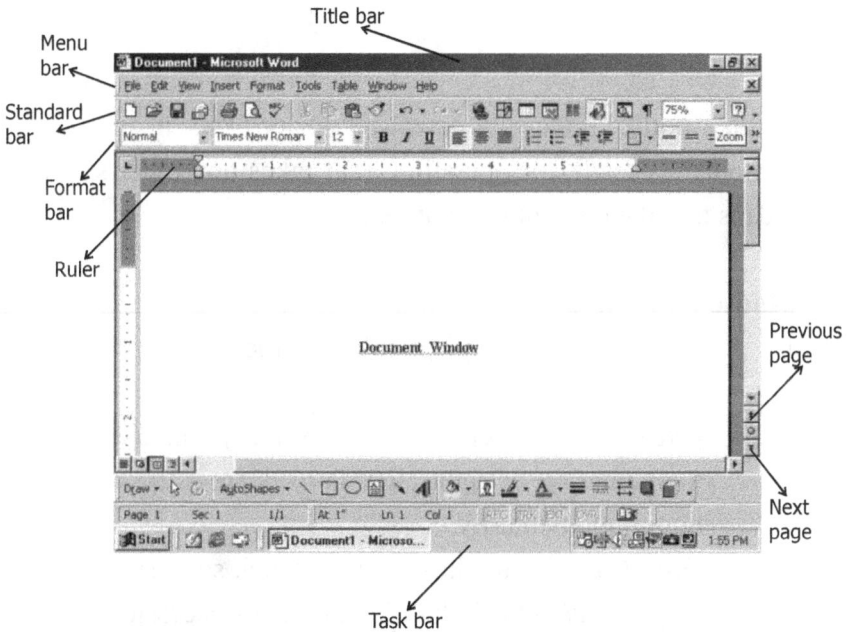

Mouse is a special input devices; it is a pointer which moves in response to movement. It also has two buttons; the primary button which is on the left, while the secondary button is on the right and a cord connecting it to the computer system's central processing unit.

Right or secondary button

Cord

Left or primary button

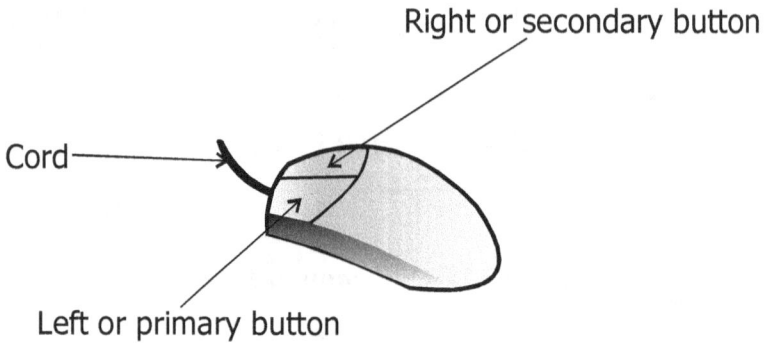

If the mouse pointer is arrowed shape ➤, it means the computer is ready for operation. If it takes any other shape, it means that the computer is not ready.

Mouse Operations:
1. *Points* – use the mouse to move the mouse pointer and place it on the desired object.
2. *Click* – to depress the primary mouse button momentarily, or right-click is to depress the secondary button momentarily.
3. *Double click* – to click twice in quick succession.
4. *Triple click* – to click thrice in quick succession.
5. *Quadruple click* – to click four times in quick succession
6. *Drag-click and drag* – means to depress mouse button, hold it down and then move the mouse on a flat surface, for instance, on a mouse pad.

Task bar – below the desktop screen in which the start button is located. The whole line is regarded as the task bar.

240

Window screen – programs and documents usually run in window screen.

Title bar **– bears the name of the program, for example, MS Word on the blue top bar, and the name of the current document.**

The program control buttons are usually located on the far right of the title bar, these are:

–   minimize button

⬚   restore/maximize button

X   close button

Minimize is used for reducing the window or screen to an icon. The **restore button** is used for reducing the window to an intermediate size while the **maximize** button is used for giving the window its maximum size.

Menu bar – contains the names of the pull-down menus on top of the screen. For example, File, Edit, View, Insert, Format, Tools, Table and Window each item on a menu represents a command.

Tool box – contains icons used for creating and editing of graphic documents.

Icons – are symbols used to represent items in windows environment. They are short-cuts.

Ruler – used for tab setting.

Colour box – contains a collection of colours which can be applied to graphic documents.

Status bar – displays information about the program and its commands. It is below the paint box and a statement-informing user of status of the toolbox is highlighted.

Document window – workspace - is the large white centrally located part of the screen. It represents the part of the screen where all data are created and edited.

Scrolls – these are vertical and horizontal bars at the right side and bottom of the document window. The scroll bars are used for displaying portions of the documents that are out of view (unseen portions).

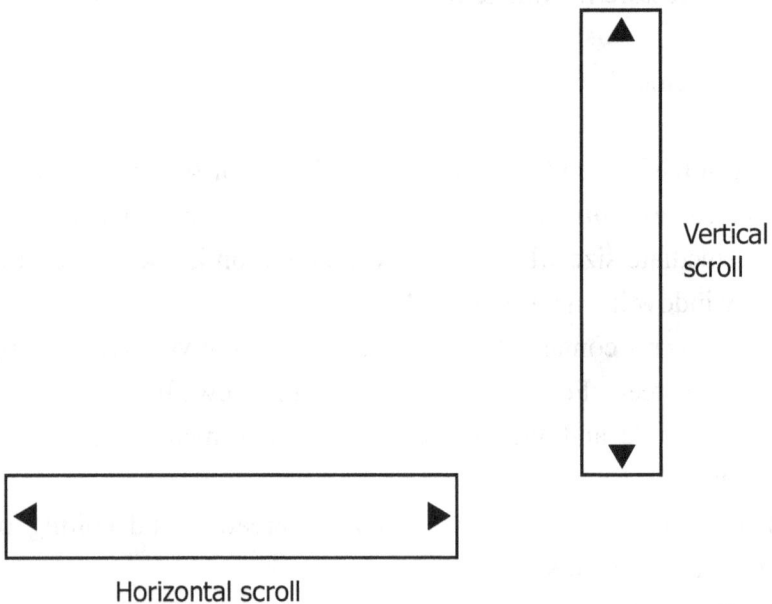

▲

▼

Vertical scroll

◄   ►

Horizontal scroll

Format bar – contains icons and are used for editing documents.

Paint – this is a graphical program used for drawing. It is one of the accessories that is supplied with widows.

To Load Paint

Steps

1.   Click Start
2.   Highlight or point to Programs
3.   Point to Accessories
4.   Click Paint

Use any shape from toolbox and click, Paint fill icon, to fill diagram and choose color.

WordPad – is used for producing documents

To Load WordPad

1.   Click Start
2.   Click programs
3.   Click Accessories
4.   Click WordPad

How to Save a Document

1.   Click the icon for Save
2.   Type the file name
3.   Click Save As in dialogue box
4.   Drop down the list labelled, Save In
5.   Click icon in front of, save in
6.   Select the desired path (destination) e.g. my documents, $3^1/_2$ Floppy (A:), or Compact Disc (E:).
7.   Click save. File name will show on the Title bar.

Clipboard – is a temporary storage facility in windows used for transferring data from one location to another.

The "copy" command or "cut" command is used for transferring data onto the clipboard. To retrieve data from the clip-board, the "paste" command is used.

To Copy Data

Click the icon for copy on the Tool bar or pull down the Edit menu and click copy.

To Cut Data

Click the icon for cut on the Tool bar or pull down Edit menu and click cut.

To Paste data from the Clipboard

Pull down the Edit menu and click Paste or click icon for paste on the tool bar.

Note: Before copying or cutting, select or highlight the relevant data.

Calculator – is one of the accessories in windows.

To Load Calculator

1.   Click Start
2.   Click Programs
3.   Click Accessories
4.   Click Calculator

There are two types of calculators:

a.   Scientific

b.   Standard

Click View and choose either standard or scientific calculator, depending on which one you need to use.

How to transfer data from one application to another, e.g. from Paint to WordPad.

To transfer a graphic from Paint to WordPad
1.   Select the data in Paint
2.   Pull down the Edit menu
3.   Click copy or cut
4.   Switch to WordPad
5.   Pull down Edit menu
6.   Click Paste

Note: To get square, press shift and rectangle circle, press shift and eclipse straight line, press shift and pencil.

To reduce diagram, move pointer to any dark point e.g. ■ and drag.

To create space between two lines, take cursor to end of first line and press Enter.

To shift a paragraph downwards, place cursor at beginning of paragraph and press Enter.

To add to table rows

Place cursor outside last row and press Enter. Or click Table, Add Row below

Microsoft Word (MW) or Ms Word

This is a word processing package developed by Microsoft Corporation.

To Load MW

1.   Click Start
2.   Click Programs
3.   Click Microsoft Word

Ms Word has a number of tool bars, each tool bar contains a collection of icons used for various purposes. Each icon has a specific function. To see the list of all the tool bars in Ms Word, pull down View menu and click Tool bars. There are sixteen of them: Standard, Formatting, Auto Text, Clipboard, Control Toolbox, Database, Drawing, Forms, Frames, Picture, Reviewing, Tables and Borders, Visual Basic, Web, Web Tools and Word Art.

To activate or deactivate a toolbar

1.   Pull down View menu
2.   Click Toolbars
3.   Click name of Toolbar required

To Open File

1.   Click Start
2.   Click Programs
3.   Click Microsoft Word
4.   Click File, Open and file name

To Close System

1.	Click lower **X** to close file after saving document, if necessary. Or pull down File menu and click close.
2.	Click upper **X** to close system
3.	Click Start
4.	Click Shutdown

Wait until the computer tells you *it is now safe to shut down your computer*.

Case Types

There are five in Ms Word

1.	*Uppercase* – all letters are capital letters.
2.	*Lowercase* – all letter are small letters.
3.	**Sentence case** – Only the first letter of a sentence is capital while others are small letters.
4.	*Title case* – first letter of each word is capital while others are small letters.
5.	*Toggle case* – every capital letter is changed to small letter and vice versa.

How to Convert or Change Case

1.	Select the text
2.	Pull down the Format menu
3.	Click Change Case
4.	Select the case type you want
5.	Click OK

How to check spellings and grammar of document

1.	Pull down the Tools menu
2.	Click Spelling and Grammar

There are six options; Ignore, Ignore All, Add, Delete, Delete All and Auto Correct. If a word occurs more than once and you know it is correct, you click Ignore All, if it is wrong, you click Change All and the computer will do that anytime the word occurs.

To put Naira Symbol (₦)
1.   Type capital N
2.   Highlight it
3.   Click Format, Font
4.   Click Double strike through
5.   Click OK

How to Save into a Diskette
1.   Pull down the File menu
2.   Click Save As
3.   Type the File name
4.   Click the icon in the box labelled Save In
5.   On the list that will appear, click $3^1/_2$ Floppy (A:)
6.   Click Save

Clipart – These are already made pictures and graphs you can paste on your document.

To insert a Clipart
1.   Pull down the Insert menu
2.   Click Picture
3.   Click Clipart
4.   Select the desired clip category
5.   Click the desired picture or graph

248

6.   Click the icon for insert clip

Tables – to insert a table
1.   Pull down Table menu
2.   Click Insert
3.   Click Table
4.   Specify the number of columns you need for your table
5.   Specify the number of rows you need
6.   If desired, select the appropriate auto fit behaviour
7.   Click OK

To Merge Cells
1.   Highlight the cells to be merged
2.   Pull down the Table menu
3.   Click merge cells

To put Gridlines in Excel
1.   Click Print Preview icon
2.   Click Setup
3.   Click Sheet
4.   Click Gridlines
5.   Click OK

To reduce spacing of typed work, e.g. double-line spacing to single-line spacing.

1.   Highlight the work
2.   Click Format
3.   Click Paragraph
4.   Click Line Spacing

5.   Click Single
6.   Click OK

If all the documents are affected
1.   Click File
2.   Click Select All
3.   Then continue with process above

Vertical Alignment of Work
1.   Click Format
2.   Click Cells (Text Direction)
3.   Click Alignment
4.   Set degree
      Change orientation degree e.g. 90%

Basic

Basic

DBMS	Data Base Management System
DOS	Diskette Operation System
DDE	Dynamic Data Exchange
CPU	Central Processing Unit
VDU	Visual Display Unit
MW/Ms	Word Microsoft Word

Bibliography

Afianmagbon, B.E. (2007), The Imperatives of Personnel Management in Vocational Education; in Babalola, J.B., Akpa, G.O. & Ayeni, A.O. (eds.) Managing Technical and Vocational Education in the Era of Globalisation. NAEAP, Nigeria. pp 47-53.

Azih, Nonye (2011), Feasibility Study Skills Required By Business Education Graduates in the Development of Entrepreneurial Skills. Association of Business Educators of Nigeria (ABEN) Vol. 1 No. 11 pp 110-116.

Babbage, C. (1832), on the Economy of Machinery and
Barnard, C.I. (1938), The functions of the Executive. Harvard Univ. Press.
    Behavior and Performance. Goodyear Publishing Co. Inc. Santa Monica, California.

Bennett, Hazel (2005), The Ultimate Teachers Handbook. Continuum International Publishing Group, New York, USA.

Buffa, E.S. (1971, Modern Production Management. John Wiley & Sons, New York.

Etzioni, Amitai (1964) Modern Organizations, Prentice Hall, Inc. Englewood Cliffs, New Jersey. Homewood, Illinois.

251

Flippo, Edwin B. (1984) Personnel Management. McGraw Hill New York, U.S.A.

ICAN (1989) Business Management Mayo - BPP, Lagos.
Koontz, H; O'Donnell, C; & Weihrich, H., (1983) Management. McGraw – Hill, London.
Manufactures, Knight, London.

Mbaezue, A.N.C. (2010), ICT and Business Education in a Globalised Economy. JTC Publishers, Enugu, Nigeria.

McCarthy, E.J., (1971) Basic Marketing. Richard D. Irwin Inc.

Osuala, E.C & Okeke, A.U. (2006) Administrative Office Management ACENA Publishers, Enugu, Nigeria.

Szilagyi, A.D. Jr.; & Wallace, M. .J. Jr.; (1980) Organizational

Tailor, F.W. (1947), Principles of Scientific Management. Harper and Brothers, N.Y.

Weber, Max (1952) in Robert K. Merton et al (eds) Reader in Bureaucracy, Glencoe, Ill. The Free Press.

Name Index

Subject Index

Problems
Bureaucratic structure
Non-Bureaucratic Head
Line and Staff relationship
Functional relationship
Customer responsibilities
Rights of the Consumer
Working capital
Microsoft word

www.ingramcontent.com/pod-product-compliance
Lightning Source LLC
Chambersburg PA
CBHW070306200326
41518CB00010B/1912